The Giant Code

Five Giants. Five Assassins. One Giant Statue

The Key to Overcoming 5 Major Temptations

Bob Blum

World rights reserved. This book or any portion thereof may not be copied or reproduced in any form or manner whatever, except as provided by law, without the written permission of the publisher, except by a reviewer who may quote brief passages in a review.

The author assumes full responsibility for the accuracy of all facts and quotations as cited in this book. The opinions expressed in this book are the author's personal views and interpretations, and do not necessarily reflect those of the publisher.

This book is provided with the understanding that the publisher is not engaged in giving spiritual, legal, medical, or other professional advice. If authoritative advice is needed, the reader should seek the counsel of a competent professional.

Copyright © 2022 Bob Blum

Copyright © 2022 TEACH Services, Inc.

ISBN-13: 978-1-4796-1447-9 (Paperback)

ISBN-13: 978-1-4796-1448-6 (ePub)

Library of Congress Control Number: 2022906284

All Scripture quotations, unless otherwise indicated, are taken from the King James Version®. Public domain.

Scripture quotations marked MKJV are taken from the Modern King James Version of the Holy Bible. Copyright © 1962–1998 by Jay P. Green, Sr. Used by permission of the copyright holder. Courtesy of Sovereign Grace Publishers and Christian Literature World. All emphasis supplied by the author.

Scripture quotations marked GW are from GOD'S WORD®, © 1995 God's Word to the Nations. Used by permission of God's Word Mission Society. All emphasis supplied by the author.

Scripture quotations marked NKJV are taken from the New King James Version®. Copyright © 1990 by Thomas Nelson. Used by permission. All rights reserved. All emphasis supplied by the author.

Scripture quotations marked BBE are taken from The Bible in Basic English. Public domain. All emphasis supplied by the author.

Scripture quotations marked GNT are from the Good News Translation in Today's English Version—Second Edition Copyright © 1992 by American Bible Society. Used by Permission. All emphasis supplied by the author.

Scripture quotations marked RSV are taken from the Revised Standard Version of the Bible. Copyright © 1946, 1952, and 1971 the Division of Christian Education of the National Council of the Churches of Christ in the United States of America. Used by permission. All rights reserved. All emphasis supplied by the author.

Scripture quotations marked LITV are taken from Green's Literal Translation. Scripture quoted by permission. Copyright 1993 by Jay P. Green Sr. All rights reserved. All emphasis supplied by the author.

TEACH Services, Inc.
PUBLISHING
www.TEACHServices.com • (800) 367-1844

CONTENTS

Introduction 5

CHAPTER 1: The Expert 12

CHAPTER 2: The Coach 22

CHAPTER 3: The Entertainer 35

CHAPTER 4: The Interpreter 47

CHAPTER 5: The Friend 68

Bibliography 112

INTRODUCTION

In Daniel 2, the king of Babylon had a dream in which he saw a fearsome giant metal image (verse 31). Daniel, a man of God, told the king that the dream portrayed five kingdoms, each greater than its follower yet less sinister, that will rule the world until the end of time. Bible scholars, for many years, have considered this prophecy as one of the most compelling arguments for the inspirational accuracy of the Bible. However, you will soon see in *The Giant Code* there are five other giant forces also portrayed here—powers everyone must personally face.

We will be looking at five giants threatening Israel in David's day that were overpowered by five of David's warriors. Among these giants were four Philistines and one Egyptian.

But, here, God goes a step further. He shows how to overcome these powers! By the time you finish this study, you will have a new concept of God's creative genius in designing His Word to completely harmonize with itself, like He did when creating our bodies.

Exposing Five Wolves in Sheep's Clothing

As with many of God's revelations to His people, the real story—the inspired one—is couched in figurative language within a believable larger story, like in Jesus' parables. And what a story these giants portray in this book! Five enemies of righteousness, worldly men of renown, are made to appear as champions for God's cause, and each time God raises up a specific defender to save the day, the king, and, perhaps, even the nation.

Early in the biblical record, giants were mentioned (Gen. 6:4). However, out of all the giants, only seven were specifically discussed. Seven? Now, that should immediately get our attention. Many times throughout the Bible, from Creation Week in Genesis to the last day apocalypse in Revelation, seven is used to show God's favor or His special involvement (Gen. 33:3; Dan 4:23). And, as you will see, it is no different when it comes to the giants in the Bible.

Whenever giants are mentioned in the Bible, they are fearful adversaries of God's kingdom. As we read about some of these giants, and break the *GIANT CODE* in which they are described, we will see pictured real adversaries we fight today—GIANT problems that we are incapable of tackling alone. But we will also see how God graciously provides victory to those with eyes that see and ears that hear.

In five of the seven giants (recorded in typical Bible *code*), we find an accurate parallel to the different powers of Nebuchadnezzar's image. In this perspective, we see the Daniel 2 image not only as depicting the worldly forces influencing and affecting God's church down through the ages but also as five major forces vying for mastery of our hearts today. Yet only here, in *THE GIANT CODE*, will we also learn what unique helps God provides to do battle with each power ... and come off the victor!

This tie-in with the oft-used prophecy of Daniel 2 underscores in bold lines that the whole Bible is, indeed, integrated and inspired and serves a common purpose—the assurance and perfection of the saints.

The Seven Giants

1. **Og, king of Bashan.** Though often referred to the most, the least is known about him. He was the only giant called a king, and usually associated with Sihon, King of the Amorites. We can only assume his size (12-13 feet tall) by reference made to his bed (4 cubits wide and 9 cubits long—Deut. 3:11). No weapons were mentioned that he might have used to provoke the children of God, and his demise was at the hand of Moses or those under his command. Since Og was a resident of the land of promise, his kingdom was divided among the sons of Gad and Reuben, and half the tribe of Manasseh (Num. 32:33). And, according to Numbers 21:35, he, his sons, and all his people were eliminated, so as not to harass God's people any more. Consequently, it doesn't appear he has a place in the kingdoms of Daniel 2. Daniel's kingdoms each had their day of power but continue to influence earthlings till the close of time. It appears Og could represent the <u>unrecorded</u> challenges to God's people, the private and personal struggles they endure, but struggles they and Christ alone must battle. The victories gained are unique and personal only, not common to the whole church, like with the last five giants.

2. **Goliath.** The most detail is given about him (1 Sam. 17). We know his name, where he grew up, his size, his weapons, his armor and what it covered and what metal was used to make it, how he provoked God's people, who killed him, and how his opponent did it. Goliath is called the father of most of the other giants that follow, and, as the "chief" of giants, represents the father of sin, the old serpent, called the devil. His challenge is accepted directly by David, a representative of Christ. This contest is a brief summary of the great controversy between Christ and Satan. We do not cover Goliath in this study, but, let me tell you, it is rich in instructive lessons (like why David used Goliath's own sword to cut off his head).

3–6. **The four "sons" of the giant.** We assume the giant mentioned as their father (or, in the Hebrew reckoning of familyhood, as the <u>chief</u> representative), was Goliath, since Og's family was obliterated. Goliath and his "sons" were all Philistines, all residents of Canaan—the land the Israelites were to inherit. But it was in God's providence that His people were to "conquer" the land, to drive out or obliterate their enemies. This was to be an object lesson to God's future Israel who were also to prepare to enter the Promised Land (new earth). Consequently, we can assume these giants represent common forces and influences God's people must face in this world and conquer (with God's help) in their personal preparation for inheriting the new earth. In this study, deliverance comes by warriors representing <u>applications of heavenly principles</u>. As we investigate them, we shall find a close parallel to the four "metal" kingdoms representing the earthly dominions from Daniel's time to the present. But Daniel was not given a "solution" to the controlling powers. That was already done, as we shall see.

7. **The Egyptian.** This fifth (and last) giant in this study is very interesting and puzzling (1 Chron. 11:23; 2 Sam. 11:23). Like the fourth "son" of the giant, he is not named. He was not a resident of the Promised Land. He wasn't defending his own turf. Simply put, he was just out of place. He apparently wasn't even connected with a band of marauders. Why he was threatening the Israelites so far from home and how he got so intimate with them is uncertain ... until we consider his counterpart. But his presence in the lineup of giants is certain. And he does help us

understand the fifth element, the clay in the feet of iron and clay kingdoms in Daniel 2, and a dimension of final victory essential to the remnant at the end of time.

We will be studying each of these five giants to understand better the masquerades and forces we contend with, some of which we are only to rest in Christ's victory, and others we are to be actively engaged in the battle. Some battles are personal, and some are fought for others.

WHAT INITIATED THIS STUDY

The inspiration for this study came from two books and an event.

The first book is the Bible itself. There I learned to read the stories like Jesus' parables. His parables were only to portray a larger story that follows the same principles. One of the first homework assignments I gave a sanctuary class was to read Matthew 13:3–23. In this parable, about twenty-three different details are given and the students were to determine which one or ones had no spiritual contribution to Christ's explanations. They could find none. The reason behind Jesus' parables and the Old Testament stories is the same: **"Because it is given unto you to know the mysteries of the kingdom of heaven, but to them it is not given"** (Matt. 13:11).

Second, a little book called *Education*, written by a popular author/speaker of the 1800s, encouraged me to not be content with a surface understanding of God's Word but to expect greater blessings by more diligent study.

> *The Bible contains all the principles that men need to understand in order to be fitted either for this life or for the life to come. And these principles may be understood by all. No one with a spirit to appreciate its teaching can read a single passage from the Bible without gaining from it some helpful thought. But the most valuable teaching of the Bible is not to be gained by occasional or disconnected study. Its great system of truth is not so presented as to be discerned by the hasty or careless reader. Many of its treasures lie <u>far beneath the surface,</u> and can be obtained only by <u>diligent research and continuous effort</u>. The truths that go to make up the great whole must be searched out and gathered up, "here a little, and there a little." Isaiah 28:10. When thus searched out and brought together, they will be found to be perfectly fitted to one another.*[1]

---

[1] Ellen G. White, *Education* (Mountain View, CA: Pacific Press, 1903), p. 123, emphasis mine.

The "event" came one time while I was reading my Bible through. I was aware that "at the mouth of two witnesses, or at the mouth of three witnesses, shall the matter be established" (Deut. 19:15), so when I came across an account of some giant battles in two different places in the Old Testament, it caught my interest. Why were these battles repeated? I started comparing them and noted some similarities and some differences. *Perhaps there's information here that could enhance spiritual life*, I mused. And thus began a several-year study on "Breaking the Giant Code."

HOW IT WAS DONE

There are four ways conclusions were made to break the "code."

1. When information was given, I first looked for other verses throughout the Bible that might help me understand what the object or name could be representing or to give me more detail on the subject. And from that data, different ideas were noted as possible solutions. This was then brought into the study. (E.g., When the weight of a spearhead was given, I looked for other places in the Bible where the same number was mentioned to see if there may be a relationship that could open up the study.)

2. If the name of the giant or a city was given, I looked up what the name might mean in the original language (using *Strong's Exhaustive Concordance of the Bible*[2]). But I also looked up other places the individual or town was mentioned in Scripture, to see what other connections it might have in the story. Then I would go to various Bible encyclopedias to hopefully gain some more insights from history or archaeology. This proved very helpful at times, like why Gath was such a popular location for both camps (Philistine and Israelites).

3. When information was not given (that I expected should be) I looked in complementary areas of the Bible to see if I could find the missing facts. If they were not to be found, I concluded it wasn't important to understand the giant or his adversary. (E.g., If a weapon was not mentioned, it was considered the giant had another agenda than to directly slay his opponent, which could be even more sinister.)

---

[2] James Strong, Dictionaries of Hebrew and Greek Words taken from Strong's Exhaustive Concordance, S.T.D., L.L.D. Published in 1890; public domain.

4. Sometimes details would lack a tie-in element, requiring me to supply one to make the study flow more smoothly. At that point, claiming James 1:5, I would seek for a word or thought that seemed practical, logical, and in harmony with the intent of 2 Tim. 3:16–17. (E.g., One giant that seems to fit the second kingdom in Nebuchadnezzar's dream is pictured in his name (in Strong's concordance) as offering God's people a shallow bowl. By harmonizing these two stories—the second giant and the second kingdom represented by silver—I took the liberty to identify the shallow bowl as one made of silver. In such instances the word or thought supplied is not given importance or significance. It was only used to help the story line.)

You'll see once you get into the different stories.

OK, let's jump in now and unwrap the GIANT CODE, that once made a mighty king so afraid.

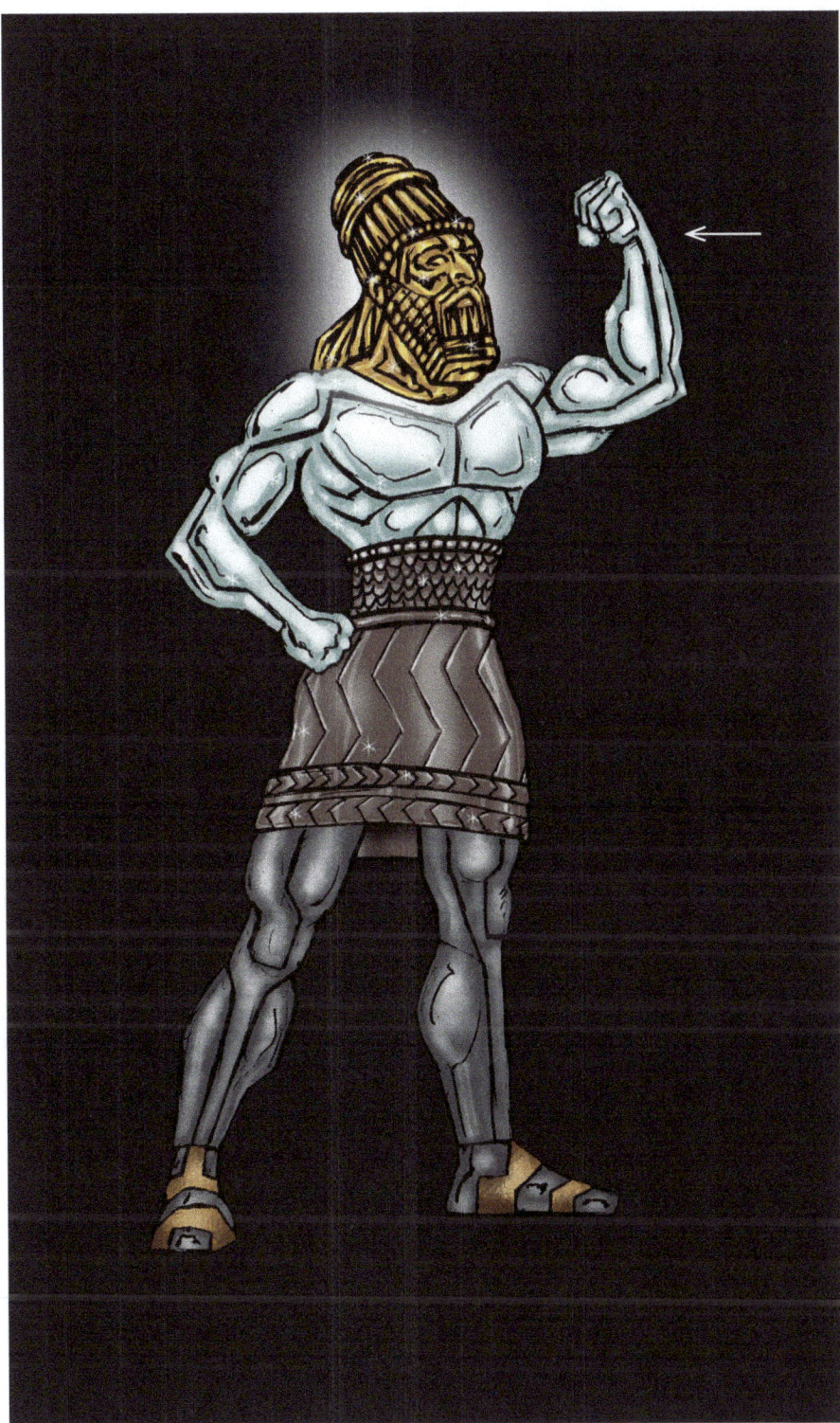

CHAPTER 1

THE EXPERT

> *"Ishbibenob, one of the sons of the giant,*
> *had a bronze spear weighing three hundred shekels.*
> *And he determined to kill David with a new sword he carried.*
> *But Abishai, the son of Zeruiah, came to his aid*
> *and struck the Philistine, and killed him."*
> 2 Samuel 21:16–17 (paraphrase)

One thing we highly value in our society are the experts. They have been there, tried this and that, had their share of failures, and finally come out successful. If only we could take advantage of their experience and save ourselves a lot of grief! Experts command a good return on their advice because it has often saved big corporations millions of dollars. And if the big boys use them, why can't we little people also? Perhaps it could get us out of the hole we have been digging for years. Yes, experts have earned their place in society.

There are experts, however, that we are cautioned against. Their advice is not favorable to God's people, though from the world's perspective many profit by them. Ishbibenob was just that type of expert—the kind God considered dangerous to His kingdom. Let's see why.

Of all the giants who threatened God's people, Ishbibenob's skills and weaponry are especially directed at leadership ("...*and he determined to kill David*" 2 Sam. 21:16, paraphrase). This threat was intended for David but represents a threat all of us should watch out for. The Bible gives several clues to this giant's identity—the first is his name.

His NAME

Names in the Bible are often descriptive of the person. Ishbibenob means "his dwelling is in Nob."[3] What is this place called Nob?

- *Nob* means fruit, germination, a cause to flourish, or to utter words that bring cheer or increase. (This gives the idea of a lush, pleasant area, with lots of fruit, and where everyone is happy.)
- *Nob* also was known as a city of priests (1 Sam. 22:19). The tabernacle was located in Nob for a period of time. David found food there when he was a fugitive fleeing from King Saul (1 Sam. 21:1–6).

So, the name of this giant associates him with abundant living: food, happiness, safety, spirituality, or whatever causes one to flourish.

Besides the giant's name, we are given other clues to his identity: his weapons, the weight of his spear, and a metal.

The Weapons

The root word for "spear" in the Bible emphasizes destruction. No question about intention here, this giant is out to kill. And he is after leadership. A sling or bow and arrow are used for defense at a distance, but a spear is used for close combat. Unless a lethal aim is certain, a spear is not usually thrown. Once out of hand, a soldier would be defenseless. Ishbibenob was an enemy designed for close combat and very adept at drawing his opponent close to himself.

The "new sword" mentioned is also a weapon for hand-to-hand conflict. However, "sword" is a supplied word. It is not in the original. All we are told is that Ishbibenob had something new he planned to use in killing David. Scholars of Old Testament language and culture say this "new" something could mean:

> *There are experts, however, that we are cautioned against. Their advice is not favorable to God's people, though from the world's perspective many profit by them. Ishbibenob was just that type of expert—the kind God considered dangerous to His kingdom. Let's see why.*

---

[3] Strong's comment on Hebrew word H3430.

- The giant may have had something tricky to fight with, something his foe didn't suspect, or perhaps didn't have experience fighting against.
- Since Ishbibenob was prepared for close combat, he might have displayed a badge or belt buckle showing his high rank and "superior" killing skill in order to intimidate his rival.
- Or it could refer to a weapon kept out of sight, like a dagger carried in a sheath between the shoulder blades.

Whatever this "new" was, we can assume it would make Ishbibenob more destructive. "New" has a fascination to us. We are drawn to it as moths to a light. It seems that if something is new, it is better, stronger, more advanced, tastier, more nutritious or healthful, more reliable and useful, faster, or of better quality. We forget, however, that the sinful heart of man often introduces a weakness in the productions of his hands or mind. The "new" genetically improved strawberry may look better and be more resistant to certain diseases, thus making a better profit, but it has lost its flavor and nutritional value (the true purpose of food). "New" technology in computer-based merchandising has made purchasing items much easier and faster at the checkout line, but it has also made us much more vulnerable and dependent on the system. When Walmart loses electricity, it quickly has the customers leave and shuts down the store. Why learn math when calculators can do our thinking for us? Why concern ourselves with proper rules of grammar or spelling when our word processors will "clean up" our letters? Why regularly schedule maintenance on our vehicles when their "idiot lights" will inform us of the proper time? Slowly, imperceptibly, we are sacrificing quality for speed, durability for lower cost, and nutrition for convenience. "New" in the hands of an enemy, can be very devastating!

Weight of His Spear

Here is the next clue. His spear weighed "three hundred shekels" (2 Sam. 21:16). In the KJV, the word "shekel" is supplied. The unit of weight is not the focus of the description for our edification here—but 300 is. Because this giant is an enemy of God's people, it is reasonable to assume the spearhead represents something also at variance with Christian principles. Whatever 300 is to the Christian, the enemy's 300 is a counterfeit. Consider these stories in which 300 played an important part for God's people.

- Enoch was translated without seeing death 300 years after the birth of his first son (Gen. 5:21–24).

- Noah and his family were saved from the great flood in an ark 300 cubits in length (Gen. 6:15).
- Joseph showed his brother Benjamin favor by a gift of 300 silver pieces, to test his brothers for jealousy. They mistook it as an omen of death (Gen. 45:22).
- Gideon's army of 32,000 was reduced to 300 before God could use them to help save His people from the Philistines (Judges 7:3–6).
- Queen Esther saw God's deliverance from Haman's evil plot and that deliverance included the death of 300 of her enemies in the palace city (Esther 9:15).
- Mary used spikenard (a relaxing, calming oil) to anoint Jesus just before His Gethsemane experience. It was valued at more than 300 pence (Mark 14:5).

Is there a pattern here? Three hundred carries the idea of <u>deliverance</u>. Though each of these has something to do with death, their associations are all with <u>a positive encounter with life</u>. Because the weight of Ishbibenob's spear was given as 300 (shekels), it appears this instrument of destruction is to be associated with <u>life and health,</u> <u>favor</u> and <u>deliverance against negative powers</u>.

This awesome giant has his own weaponry to fight the battles of life … and he gets results—wonderful results. Problems fall by the wayside. Successes pierce any difficulty. And it is obvious that a power greater than man is involved. But remember, this giant is an enemy, and every description of his person or weaponry is intended to expose his evils!

The Metal

Brass was the metal of choice for Ishbibenob's weapon. Since <u>brass</u> is not found in nature, man must put it together from other natural metals. Wherever brass is used in Scripture, the connection is with <u>something on earth</u> or something <u>involving</u> <u>mankind</u>. These aren't necessarily bad happenings or things, just human or earth-oriented.

A good weapon, if we know how to use it, can make us feel more in control and less fearful when threatened by man or beast. Since the giant's spear was made of brass, we can assume it represents putting confidence in what <u>man can do to protect himself</u>. And because we are describing an enemy of God's people, it would indicate a God-less, humanistic approach. "Man-made solutions" rather than God-made ones.

The deliverance, then, mentioned above would come as a result of *human* planning, *human* devising, *human* logic, *human* effort, but the results would appear **parahuman** (where human power is working alongside a higher power). Ishbibenob says, *"You can do whatever you want to do. The power is within you. All you have to do is focus that power, and I have just the thing to do it! Come close and I will show you."* He thus lures us into his deceptive power like he did Eve at the tree of knowledge of good and evil.

PUTTING IT ALL TOGETHER

So, there he is, a gigantic enemy, skilled, equipped, and determined to bring down leaders of God's people. What makes him so treacherous? He lives in vales of luxury and prosperity. He appears victorious over every earthly challenge. And he always has something new and exciting to draw us to himself.

We can think of the Philistine camp as Satan's enchanted playground. It's designed to allure and destroy.

The weight of the spearhead (300) and the metal it is made from (brass) exposes one of Satan's most frightening giants—the EXPERT—bringing with him prosperity, deliverance, success, and favor. His real identity? SELF SUFFICIENCY. This giant raves, *"Deliver yourself by the powers inherent in you. Gain success by my human methods. Look at me! Make yourself rich and famous like I have done. You can do it! Come into my lair and I will show you how."*

Prosperity's golden finger is used to exterminate God's people. Satan has learned over the years that what persecution cannot silence, success and prosperity can.

And this doesn't have to be just worldly entertainment or business practices. It can also include any perversion of God's blessings, including church growth. The tree we were not supposed to eat of was called the tree of knowledge of good and evil. That is some evil mixed in with good. It doesn't have to be much, even. Perhaps not even noticeable (at first).

We have been conditioned from infancy to think of prosperity, deliverance, success, and favor as always positive. Only a fool would turn his back on these! But consider the counsel of God.

"An Ammonite or Moabite shall not enter into the congregation of the LORD .... You shall not seek their peace nor their prosperity all your days forever" (Deut. 23:3,6, NKJV).

"I spoke to you in your prosperity; but you said, I will not hear. This has been your way from your youth, for you have not obeyed My voice" (Jer. 22:21, MKJV).

And read David's lament in Psalm 73:1–16 (GW Version):

> God is truly good to Israel, to those whose lives are pure. But my feet had almost stumbled. They had almost slipped because I was envious of arrogant people when I saw the prosperity that wicked people enjoy.
>
> They suffer no pain. Their bodies are healthy. They have no drudgery in their lives like ordinary people. They are not plagued with problems like others. That is why they wear arrogance like a necklace and acts of violence like clothing. Their eyes peer out from their fat faces, and their imaginations run wild. They ridicule. They speak maliciously. They speak arrogantly about oppression. They verbally attack heaven, and they order people around on earth. That is why God's people turn to wickedness and swallow their words.
>
> Then wicked people ask, "What does God know?" "Does the Most High know anything?" Look how wicked they are! They never have a worry. They grow more and more wealthy. I've received no reward for keeping my life pure and washing my hands of any blame. I'm plagued with problems all day long, and every morning my punishment begins again. If I had said, "I will continue to talk like that," I would have betrayed God's people. But when I tried to understand this, it was too difficult for me.

David's envying of the prosperous almost caused him to lose his hold on God. It almost destroyed the king of Israel.

Pride often follows closely on the heels of prosperity. It definitely had its effect on the king of Babylon. Remember Nebuchadnezzar's boast before he lost his sanity? **"Is not this great Babylon, that I have built?"** (Dan. 4:30).

IS PROSPERITY EVIL, THEN?

Let's not confuse all prosperity with evil. It is God's purpose to prosper His people, to shower them with deliverance that gives abundant life, favors, and health.

"And his master saw that the LORD was with him, and that the LORD made all that he did to prosper in his hand" (Gen. 39:3).

The God of creation desires to prosper His people. But there is a stipulation. And once that stipulation is an integral part of our thinking and belief system, there is no limit to what God can give us.

What does God need in order to prosper us? Let's look at the one who killed Ishbibenob.

GOD'S DELIVERER

Abishai, one of David's great warriors, knew how to wield a spear and had his own 300. (A note of interest here. Each warrior who does battle with the different giants is designed by God to have similar characteristics as the enemy he fights—only with a divine twist.)

"Joab's brother Abishai, Zeruiah's son, was the leader of the thirty. He used his spear to kill 300 men. He was as famous as the three and was honored more than they were. So he became their captain, but he didn't become a member of the three" (2 Sam. 23:18–19, GW).

When David was a fugitive, he and Abishai came across the sleeping Saul and his guards. Abishai wanted to thrust his spear through the renegade king, but David's whisper forbade him. Though mighty, Abishai was able to take orders.

These commendable attributes, however, were not the focus of his success against the giant that day. No weapons or strategies are referred to in describing the one who succeeded in overcoming this powerful foe. All that is mentioned as a qualifier to do battle against Ishbibenob was the deliverer's name and the name of his mother!

- Abishai: the father of a gift, generous.
- Zeruiah: wounded or cracked by pressure or by distillation, as in making balm.

The picture comes through. Zeruiah, one of David's sisters,[4] had gone through very trying circumstances, but came out on top. When the pressure bore down on her, she did not crumble. By the grace of God, she became as a fragrant ointment or aromatic oil for healing or anointing. Her example apparently impressed her son, Abishai, for his name characterizes empathy toward those in need. Abishai knew what it meant to suffer, apparently by observing his mother, and was eager to help others in need.

It is this very combination—generosity rising out of hardship or generosity resulting from an understanding of the pain of others—that

---
[4] 1 Chronicles 2:16.

overcomes the evils of prosperity. To a heart longing to help others, prosperity and wealth become a means to bless them. To a heart focused on self, riches and honor take on silent, destructive forces.

David also suffered much, but he had a difficult time with prosperity. Suffering alone is not sufficient to overcome the specter of prosperity; it must be accompanied with generosity, using gifts entrusted to us to bless the lives of those less fortunate. Notice the counsel Daniel gave the mighty king of Babylon—the head of gold—the one who represented prosperity at its highest:

"Therefore, O king, let my advice be pleasing to you, and break off your sins by righteousness, and your iniquities by showing mercy to the poor, whether there will be duration to your prosperity" (Dan. 4:27, MKJV).

Note also the implications in Jesus' parable of the rich landowner:

"And he said unto them, Take heed, and beware of covetousness: for a man's life consisteth not in the abundance of the things which he possesseth" (Luke 12:15).

Then he used this illustration:

> **The ground of a certain rich man brought forth plentifully:**
>
> **And he thought within himself, saying, What shall I do, because I have no room where to bestow my fruits? And he said, This will I do: I will pull down my barns, and build greater; and there will I bestow all my fruits and my goods. And I will say to my soul, Soul, thou hast much goods laid up for many years; take thine ease, eat, drink, and be merry.**
>
> **But God said unto him, Thou fool, this night thy soul shall be required of thee: then whose shall those things be, which thou hast provided?**
>
> **So is he that layeth up treasure for himself, and is not rich toward God.** (Luke 12:16–21)

Jesus did not denounce the man for his wealth, but rather what he did with it. Wealth, fame, influence, and talent cannot harm the soul that ever remembers he is a <u>steward</u> of God's blessings—to do good to others—and not an owner of them. God must be able to pour the riches of heaven and earth <u>through</u> us, not just <u>in</u> us to be used for and on ourselves. It is only when we become channels—not holding tanks—that we are out of danger.

Babylon, the golden kingdom, still has a strong influence on nations, leaders, and the church. Her experts on prosperity are all over the world and are a great threat to saints today, in that their advice feeds self-sufficiency and self-absorption. Wherever we turn, whether to education, ministry, business, or healthful living, the world lures us to itself, promising success and security, and appearing very much an example of its claims. Yet God's Word sounds a warning. With a heart devoted to help and bless those in need, and our confidence in God's loving, providential care, the Expert's power is broken!

And God, the El Shaddai, the God of "more than enough," can abundantly prosper His people without it harming them. This is His first choice.

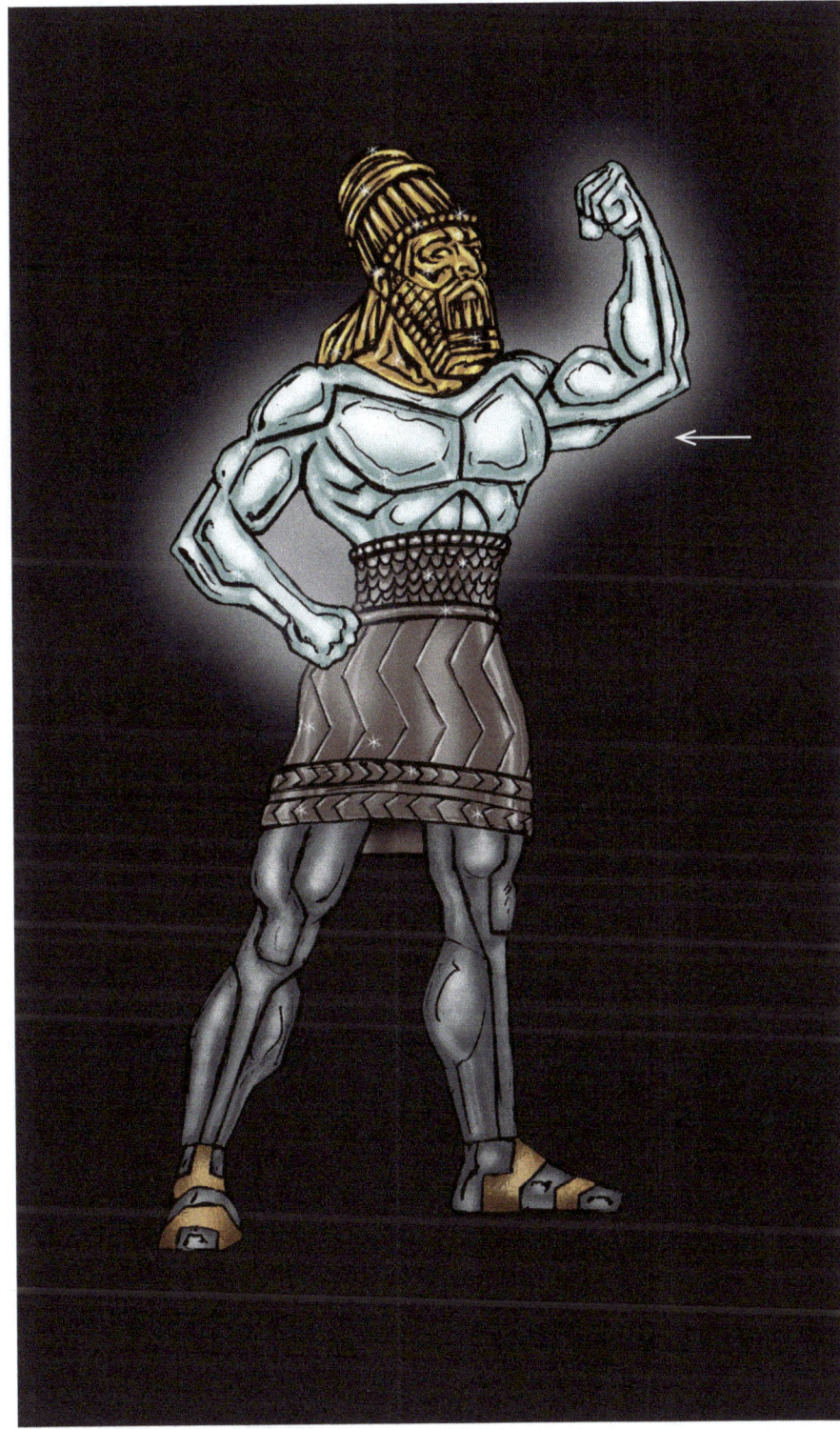

CHAPTER 2

THE COACH

*"And it happened after this
there was again a battle with the Philistines at Gob.
Then Sibbechai the Hushathite
killed Saph,
who was of the sons of the giant."*

2 Samuel 21:18 (MKJV)

There is another type of advisor we are attracted to: The Coach. The Expert is just that—an expert. It is pretty much up to us as to how we shall integrate his counsel. But the Coach is a step closer. He is a hands-on teacher—right there with us, watching every move, commending us when we perform well and advising us how to do this better and why we should do that. He is there at our first lesson and there when we graduate. Though we may highly respect the knowledge of the Experts, it's the Coaches whom we soon call by their first name. To us their word is gospel.

★ ★ ★ ★

With the second giant that threatened the "light of Israel," no mention is made of weapons or armament, just the place of battle and his name. The omission of a weapon leads us to think that this giant was not to be feared for his destructive powers but something else. What is there to be afraid of if it will not kill?

This giant was also a champion of the Philistines. He, too, symbolized some aspect of worldliness, some characteristic of those who pit themselves against divine authority. Whatever he represents, we can be certain his presence in the life will distract our relationship with God and our service for Him, bringing confusion, discord, disruption, and impotence. If the quality of life is important to us, besides life itself, then annihilating this leviathan is critical!

THE PLACE OF BATTLE

The battle, we are told, was at Gob (2 Sam. 21:18–19), also called Gezer (1 Chron. 20:4)—a place in western Palestine, home territory to the tribe of Ephraim. But Ephraim did not drive out the Canaanites as God commanded. Instead, they kept the Canaanites as "servants."

"And they did not drive out the Canaanites who lived in Gezer. But the Canaanites live among the Ephraimites until this day, and serve under tribute" (Joshua 16:10, MKJV).

Had they extricated them as directed, this giant would not have been a threat, nor this battle necessary. There are many difficulties we face because of disobedience. It is a fearful thing to play with evil, to think we can control or harness it for personal advantage. King Saul thought he could by sparing Agag, the king of the Amalekites, as well as the best of the spoil, though ordered to destroy absolutely everything:

> **"Saul and the army spared Agag and the best sheep and cows, the fattened animals, the lambs, and all the best property. The army refused to claim them for God by destroying them. But everything that was worthless and weak the army did claim for God and destroy"** (1 Sam. 15:9, GW).

When Samuel asked Saul why he did not obey the Lord, Saul claimed he saved the best to use as an offering for the Lord. Apparently, the king thought evil could be contained and its "benefits" used in the worship of God. This was a fatal mistake,[5] costing him his position as king and possibly his soul.

> **"Samuel said, 'Which does the LORD prefer: obedience or offerings and sacrifices? It is better to obey him than to sacrifice the best sheep to him. Rebellion against him is as bad as witchcraft, and arrogance is as sinful as idolatry. Because you rejected the LORD's command, he has rejected you as king'"** (1 Sam. 15:22–23, GNT).

We would do well to examine our own lives to see if we have compromised with evil, if we have kept back only the choicest parts of worldliness and sin. Perhaps in our business dealings we have taken advantage of others

---
[5] King Agag and all Amalekites hated God's people and vowed to destroy them.

and used portions of our "profits" for mission work. God can bless a widow's honest mite but not ill-gotten gain. Or maybe we try to justify a sharp tongue or believe an intemperate lifestyle has some merit. God, help us!

If Ephraim had obeyed the Lord and driven out the Canaanites, would Saph have been a concern?

HIS NAME

The lack of weapon description is not the only indication we have of this giant's purpose. We see it also in his name. Saph (or Sippai in 1 Chron. 20:4) has in its original sense the idea of containing something, like a dish or bowl. We don't want to offend such a nice and commanding individual. (Remember, the Ephraimites saw some "advantage" in keeping these Canaanites around as servants.)

But there is more to his name. We also find that the idea of containment is accompanied with a little parenthetical phrase, "as a limit." And the root word means properly, "to snatch away." The bowl Saph offers is a shallow one; the dish is a small one. We are flattered that this important person is offering us a container for our food. But because it does not hold much, we walk *away, content* with little, leaving the greater portion of God's blessings to spoil behind us.

Saph is the Philistine champion we call THE COACH, the one who sets the limits. What makes his work so hard to detect is that the whole economy of heaven and earth is laced and interlaced with limits of all kinds. Look over the list below and see if there are not limits—natural and otherwise—established for our good.

The Ten Commandments

Traffic laws

Budgets

Desserts

Lusts of the flesh

Time

Human strength

Jungle paths

Principles of health

Oceans, seas, and all bodies of water

So, why make a big thing about Saph? Simply because there are times when God wants us to be free to think, create, express, and do, and the Coach thwarts God's gracious purposes by his crafty reasonings and immutable laws. Observe how he works. Below are two perspectives of the same story.

While at a feast in Jesus' honor, Mary, a very sensitive and devoted follower, out of great love for her Savior, has just anointed Jesus with a very costly (and aromatic) oil. Her act of devotion was severely criticized, however. In this first reference (Mark 14:3–8) it appears several guests at the feast were concerned and thought such extravagance should be censored. The equivalent of a year's wages could greatly benefit the worthy poor. Their logic appeared faultless. The sting of condemnation went straight to Mary's heart, bringing confusion and embarrassment.

> **And being in Bethany in the house of Simon the leper, as He reclined, a woman came with an alabaster vial of pure, costly ointment of spikenard. And she broke the vial and poured it on His head. And some were indignant to themselves, and said, Why was this waste of the ointment made? For it might have been sold for more than three hundred denarii, and be given to the poor. And they were incensed with her.** (Mark 14:3–5, MKJV)

John, on the other hand, tells the story from a slightly different perspective (John 12:3–7). He identifies the Coach—and it wasn't a group of concerned disciples championing the cause of the poor!

> **Then Mary took a pound of ointment of pure spikenard, very costly, and anointed the feet of Jesus, and wiped His feet with her hair. And the house was filled with the odor of the ointment. Then said one of His disciples (Judas Iscariot, Simon's son, who was to betray Him) Why was this ointment not sold for three hundred denarii and given to the poor? He said this, not that he cared for the poor, but because he was a thief and held the moneybag and carried the things put in. Then Jesus said, Let her alone. She has kept this for the day of My burial.** (John 12:3–7, MKJV)

Next to Jesus, Judas was the disciple all the others looked up to and trusted. He had education, prestige, influence. He knew how the world worked. And he had a way with words. But he had Saph's heart!

Saph's object is to rob us of an experience with God and make us feel He is exacting and selfish and conniving. The Philistine's shallow bowls are offered when God wants us to have deep bowls and large plates. Just when the Lord wishes us to drink freely of His waters, venture much for

His cause, enjoy the pleasures of His touch, or increase our capacities for service in His kingdom, Saph intrudes himself and smooth talks us into holding back or tries to confine us by man-made laws.

An example of the latter is from a chapter in Esther's life.

> **And Haman said unto king Ahasuerus, There is a certain people scattered abroad and dispersed among the people in all the provinces of thy kingdom; and their laws are diverse from all people; neither keep they the king's laws: therefore it is not for the king's profit to suffer them. If it please the king, let it be written that they may be destroyed: and I will pay ten thousand talents of silver to the hands of those that have the charge of the business, to bring it into the king's treasuries. And the king took his ring from his hand, and gave it unto Haman the son of Hammedatha the Agagite, the Jews' enemy. (Esther 3:8–10)**

Note that this was a Medo-Persian kingdom (Esther 1:3); the king was tricked into an agreement which he could not retract, and the bribe was in the form of SILVER. Now look at the king's response when he learned of the deception and what he had to do to grant lovely Esther's request.

> **And said, If it please the king, and if I have favour in his sight, and the thing seem right before the king, and I be pleasing in his eyes, let it be written to reverse the letters devised by Haman the son of Hammedatha the Agagite, which he wrote to destroy the Jews which are in all the king's provinces: for how can I endure to see the evil that shall come unto my people? or how can I endure to see the destruction of my kindred? Then the king Ahasuerus said unto Esther the queen and to Mordecai the Jew, Behold, I have given Esther the house of Haman, and him they have hanged upon the gallows, because he laid his hand upon the Jews. Write ye also for the Jews, as it liketh you, in the king's name, and seal it with the king's ring: for the writing which is written in the king's name, and sealed with the king's ring, may no man reverse. (Esther 8:5–8)**

Because the king could not reverse his edict (to destroy the Jews), he gave permission to write another edict to counteract the first one (that the Jews could defend themselves with the king's support).

Limiting may not destroy the church of God, but it can definitely weaken her influence and delay her work if she falls for Saph's schemes. God, help us to be watchful and prayerful, as was Esther and Mordecai!

Worldly schemes, worldly policies, worldly methods—all are directed at leadership to limit the effectiveness of God's kingdom on this earth. It all sounds so good. Because we see no obvious weapon in Saph's hand, we assume he is harmless or friendly, and we do not raise a standard against him. And in the end, both we and God's work suffer.

Listed below are a few of the ways Saph tries to restrict the kingdom of God besides legal enactments.

1. UNNECESSARY CAUTION

When Christ appeared to His disciples after the resurrection, Thomas was not in the midst. Their enthusiasm and excitement were dampened by Thomas's caution. **"Except I shall see in his hands the print of the nails, and put my finger into the print of the nails, and thrust my hand into his side, I will not believe"** (John 20:25). Thomas missed a great blessing and later received a chastisement from the Lord: **"[B]lessed are they that have not seen, and yet have believed"** (verse 29).

2. EARTHLY TREASURES

In the early history of the New Testament church, needs were great, and it was not uncommon for believers to sacrifice for the cause. There were two disciples, Ananias and Sapphira, who let earthly treasures limit their giving. It did not turn out well. You can read the story in Acts 5.

3. WITHDRAWING FROM THOSE WHO THINK DIFFERENTLY

The classic example here is how the Pharisees withdrew from their Messiah because He didn't fit into their traditional expectations. **"The officers answered, Never man spake like this man. Then answered them the Pharisees, Are ye also deceived? Have any of the rulers or of the Pharisees believed on him?"** (John 7:46–48).

4. STINGY, MISERLY PEOPLE

God does not entrust His important work to those who think it more important to save money than to help those in need. They would grudge the smallest pittance to the needy in their distress. Their money would be more valuable to them than precious souls for whom Christ died. An extreme example is the farmer who thought only of himself, even in his abundance (Luke 12:16–21).

5. IDLENESS

We are standing on the very threshold of eternity, and we need to realize the claims God has upon us to do something, and do it now. If we fold our hands in idleness, we give expression to a weak, unbelieving faith. The measure of our faith is proportional to our fervor. If we have a mind to work, and do so trusting in Jesus for help and wisdom, we shall see great things accomplished. **"Go to the ant, thou sluggard; consider her ways, and be wise: which having no guide, overseer, or ruler, provideth her meat in the summer, and gathereth her food in the harvest. How long wilt thou sleep, O sluggard? when wilt thou arise out of thy sleep? Yet a little sleep, a little slumber, a little folding of the hands to sleep: so shall thy poverty come as one that travelleth, and thy want as an armed man"** (Prov. 6:6–11).

6. UNWISE MOVES

Many a battle has been lost by unwise moves. Many a fortune has been forfeited by limited thinking. The work of God must move forward and at some time with great speed and sacrifice. To always consider approaching the future with shallow bowls, with cautious, limited thinking could cause great loss to God's cause, as well as an important family or business venture. A refreshing yet sad story is found in 1 Samuel 14, contrasting the limitless faith of a son and the limited fear of a father. I highly suggest you read it.

Brian Sauder, in his book, *Prosperity with a Purpose*, shares in the opening chapter an enlightening example of how the Coach can affect even our giving to missions. The book is a Christian's perspective on prosperity, God's first choice for His people. He explains how he thought restricting his family to eating just rice and beans for a month would allow them to give more for missions. His wife objected. These are his afterthoughts:

> *I was not believing that God could supply more for us so that we could give more. In my thinking, we were limited to my paycheck. I looked at the income we had and saw that as a ceiling rather than believing God for more money. So I wanted to take food from my children's mouths and give it to missions. What picture of God the Father does that give to my children? It shows them He is a stingy Father, who gives us just enough or barely enough to survive. As we will explore in this book, this is not a biblically accurate picture of God. I realized it was not right for me to show my children this tainted portrayal of God.*[6]

---

[6] Brian Sauder, *Prosperity with a Purpose* (House to House Publications, 2003), p. 14.

Saph has many ways to limit the work when God intends it to go forward. Our leaders are especially vulnerable, and it is up to us to help and encourage them, as Sibbechai did for King David.

SAPH'S COUNTERPART IN DANIEL 2

As we turn back to Daniel, we will look at the second kingdom in Nebuchadnezzar's giant image, the one represented by silver, the Medo-Persian empire. Here are some texts on this kingdom.

- "[H]is breast and his arms of silver [the second kingdom]" (Dan. 2:32).
- "And after thee [Babylon, the head of gold] **shall arise another kingdom inferior to thee**" (Dan. 2:39).
- "**Thy kingdom is divided, and given to the Medes and Persians** [the second kingdom identified]" (Dan. 5:28).

The second kingdom in the giant image was represented by silver, an element inferior to gold as Medo-Persia was inferior to Babylon. Do we see any characteristics of Saph, the Coach, here? We certainly do! Besides the experience mentioned in Esther, we see another one early in Daniel 6. The presidents and princes of whom the king set Daniel above were jealous of this Jewish exile ruling over them. Knowing that Daniel faithfully and openly prayed to his God several times a day, they tricked the king to make a proclamation, as Haman did with King Ahasuarus.

> **Then said these men, We shall not find any occasion against this Daniel, except we find it against him concerning the law of his God. Then these presidents and princes assembled together to the king, and said thus unto him, King Darius, live for ever. All the presidents of the kingdom, the governors, and the princes, the counsellors, and the captains, have consulted together to establish a royal statute, and to make a firm decree, that whosoever shall ask a petition of any God or man for thirty days, save of thee, O king, he shall be cast into the den of lions. Now, O king, establish the decree, and sign the writing, that it be not changed, according to the law of the Medes and Persians, which altereth not. Wherefore king Darius signed the writing and the decree.** (Dan. 6:5–9)

It was the law of the Medes and Persians, the silver kingdom, that whatever was signed by the king could not be altered—even if he were tricked into signing it! Look how this played out in Daniel's case.

> **Then these men assembled, and found Daniel praying and making supplication before his God. Then they came near, and spake before the king concerning the king's decree; Hast thou not signed a decree, that every man that shall ask a petition of any God or man within thirty days, save of thee, O king, shall be cast into the den of lions? The king answered and said, The thing is true, according to the law of the Medes and Persians, which altereth not. Then answered they and said before the king, That Daniel, which is of the children of the captivity of Judah, regardeth not thee, O king, nor the decree that thou hast signed, but maketh his petition three times a day. Then the king, when he heard these words, was sore displeased with himself, and set his heart on Daniel to deliver him: and he laboured till the going down of the sun to deliver him. Then these men assembled unto the king, and said unto the king, Know, O king, that the law of the Medes and Persians is, That no decree nor statute which the king establisheth may be changed. Then the king commanded, and they brought Daniel, and cast him into the den of lions.** (Dan. 6:11–16)

The king realized he was bound by his own laws so much that, try as he might, he could not save his friend Daniel. He had to cast him into the den of lions. God, however, was not bound by these human enactments. He delivered His faithful son—much to the joy of the king.

Here we see how powerful the Coach can work to accomplish his aim (to constrain God's work on this earth through His faithful followers). If he cannot kill, like his brother Ishbibenob, he will try to enslave by human enactments. Christians do not need to be overpowered by the Coach!

DAVID'S VULNERABILITY

David, though a man after God's own heart, was overcome at times by human weakness. Whether his vulnerability came from pride, lust, or discouragement, it still affected his ability to fight. During these times, he especially needed the support and help of his faithful soldiers.

Prior to Saph's encounter with the mighty warrior of God, we read of an incident in David's life that opened the door of vulnerability. It is recorded in 1 Chronicles 20:1. Note the two underlined sections in the paragraph following the verse.

"**And it happened after the year had ended, at the time kings go forth. Joab led out the power of the army and wasted the country of the sons of Amman. And he came and besieged Rabbah. But David staved (tarried)** at Jerusalem. And Joab struck Rabbah and destroyed it" (1 Chron. 20:1, MKJV).

When the king <u>should have been with his forces</u>, he tarried in the capital city. When he should have been encouraging and leading his warriors, <u>he allowed himself to be distracted</u>. In 2 Samuel 11, we are told what he was doing when he should have been defending his country. The sin he got trapped in left him helpless and defenseless when Saph appeared.

> **And it happened at the turn of the year, at the time kings go forth, David sent Joab, and his servants with him, and all Israel. And they destroyed the sons of Amman and circled Rabbah. But David remained at Jerusalem. And it happened one evening, David arose from his bed and walked on the roof of the king's house. And from the roof he saw a woman bathing. And the woman was very beautiful to look upon.** (2 Sam. 11:1–2, MKJV)

Our leaders are ever beset by temptations, for Satan knows that if he can get them to fall, it will be easier for us to follow. It is during these times, when our supervisors, managers, pastors, or elders have, by disobedience, temporarily laid aside their armor that we need to come to their rescue. Instead of accusations, criticism, and defamation, we need to take up the battle ourselves and help them through it. Though David opened himself up to temptation, Sibbechai was there when the enemy came in like a flood. Who was this soldier? What qualified him to do battle with the Coach, the champion of the Philistines, and the silver kingdom?

SIBBECHAI, THE HUSHATHITE

His name in Hebrew means "copse-like." The root from which this comes is interpreted as "to entwine:—fold together, wrap." What is it that he joins or weaves together? A copse is a thicket of small trees or shrubs. Trees have always **represented people**—the righteous (Ps. 1:3) and wicked (Ps. 37:35), kings (Dan. 4:20–23) and countrymen (Judges 9:8). A thicket of small trees, then, would be either a group of young people ("small" relating to age) or those who have not reached a prominent position in life ("small" relating to social status). Sibbechai must have had a charisma to draw these special people together. He must have known how to entwine their petulant and restless spirits into a common good. But we know more about him.

He also was a Hushathite, those who were in haste, those eager with excitement or enjoyment. The group under his supervision, whether they be youth or "small" people, were not a sit-back group. Sebbechai was a leader with enthusiasm, animation, and exhilaration. And those he led likely would follow with the same. Wherever Sebbechai went, anticipation was high.

We also understand from 1 Chronicles 27:11 that he was "of the Zarhites." Zerah was of the tribe of Judah (Num. 26:20). Zerah's name signified "a rising of light," "a shooting forth beams of light." And to the Hebrew, light was ever a representation of God, His Word, or His kingdom. This tribe represented energy big-time! Judah, from whose bowels they all descended, adds the concept of praise and thanksgiving.

Sibbechi believed in God, whose truths were as lamps to his feet and light to his paths. His enthusiastic love for God and appreciation for all that God had done for him, inspired his group. Wherever he went, he cast no shadows. And Sibbechai loved "little" people. Though they were "small" (perhaps young in the faith, humble, insignificant in their own eyes), there was nothing they could not do with God's help. Perhaps this was why his legion of 24,000 soldiers was given the eighth position among the twelve captains who rotated command one month out of the year at Jerusalem (1 Chron. 27). The Hebrew word for "eight" gives the idea of plumpness, as if a surplus above the "perfect" seven. In all this, do you get any intimation of <u>faithless</u> limiting? This is the one who slew Saph.

David's sin with Bathsheba had weakened the warrior for God—at least to the point that he could not fight the Coach. But the one God personally designed to do battle with him prevailed and came off victor. David was saved. Israel was saved. And God's kingdom advanced.

> *In the spirit of Sibbechai, with your eye on the Sun of Righteousness, your heart filled with thanksgiving, your soul fired with zeal for God's kingdom, appeal to the "little ones," those who are small in their own eyes but full of faith in Christ's power to save, and together raise a standard against the Coach.*

Do you hear Saph's sweet voice in your church planning committees or missionary ventures or evangelistic programs? Do you see the shallow bowl handed around for advancing God's kingdom or the tiny plate offered to collect funds for the needed church school? Do you sense THE COACH's presence in your home or place of business holding you back from a faith-oriented life? "It's too costly or ill-timed or appears too legalistic or the effort is better directed toward a more "acceptable" cause," he says.

Don't think Saph's lack of weapons makes him harmless! He is a powerful enemy and must be brought down without mercy. God's kingdom is at stake! (There will be no Saphs in the Promised Land.) In the spirit of Sibbechai, with your eye on the Sun of Righteousness, your heart filled with thanksgiving, your soul fired with zeal for God's kingdom, appeal to the "little ones," those who are small in their own eyes but full of faith in Christ's power to save, and together raise a standard against the Coach. To this, if you are obedient, the Coach is powerless to thwart your service or devotion to God, and you will not be distracted by the world's glitter nor powerful laws.

CHAPTER 3

THE ENTERTAINER

"And there was war again with the Philistines; and Elhanan the son of Jair slew [Lahmi] the brother of Goliath the Gittite, whose spear staff was like a weaver's beam."

1 Chronicles 20:5

Mark Twain once said, "Against the assault of laughter nothing can stand."[7] Laughter does seem to be a powerful weapon against many stresses and pressures of life, and, some claim, even cancers.[8] It, laughter therapists say, is the human gift for coping[9] and sometimes even survival. "Research … published in 2015, found evidence of a link between happiness and productivity. One of the techniques used in his study was to use comedy to make participants laugh and be happier."[10] The posted results were that it boosted productivity by up to 12 percent.[11]

The Entertainer takes advantage of all these, to make you feel good … but with ill fortune in mind. WATCH OUT!

It was the purpose of God that the Israelites should, in His name and power, claim the Promised Land for themselves, clearing it of all their enemies. Their experience was to be a type of our experience as we also

---

[7] Holger Kersten, JSTOR, https://1ref.us/1sa (accessed November 17, 2021).
[8] Lynn Erdman, Laughter Therapy for Patients with Cancer, Taylor & Francis Online, https://1ref.us/1sb (accessed November 17, 2021).
[9] Enda Junkins, "Welcome to Laughter Therapy Enterprises," Laughter Therapy Enterprises, https://1ref.us/1sc (accessed November 17, 2021).
[10] Vicky McKeever, "Why laughter can make you more productive at work," CNBC, https://1ref.us/1sd (accessed November 17, 2021).
[11] Ibid.

> *God's remnant Israel, in the last days, must reclaim His inheritance, fighting anew the giants that once threatened the kingdoms of old. Scripture has preserved the confrontations so we may know how to fight, or who to let fight, the battles.*

prepare to enter the Promised Land. The problems they faced, we face. The giants they encountered, we encounter. The victories they gained, we can also gain. Presently, we are studying the fiends that threatened the kingdom under David's reign.

In the reigns of the sweet singer and his son, Solomon, Israel reached the height of her greatness. It was during this rise into national and spiritual prosperity that we see some of Israel's greatest challenges and victories. Had God's people added faith to faith, history would have been much different. The sad record of Israel's apostasy and losses due to sin would never have been written. But they failed to fulfill God's promises for them, promises that are still viable today. So, God's remnant Israel, in the last days, must reclaim His inheritance, fighting anew the giants that once threatened the kingdoms of old. Scripture has preserved the confrontations so we may know how to fight, or who to let fight, the battles.

THE BATTLE IN GOB

In the previous study, we learned that Gob was a place in Palestine, the home of God's people. Here was a struggle to clean up the very heart of the nation. This battle with Lahmi was because the enemy came TO them. How he got there we are not told. Whether he forced his way in through a weak defense, or stole in while the guardians slept, or disguised himself in some attractive form and was invited in, we do not know. The story begins only at the point of obvious awareness of his threat to the kingdom.

So it is today. Each of us may face the same giants, though the reason for having the battle may be different. Perhaps we were distracted, or slept, or beguiled by some worldly attraction. The point of greatest concern now is this: How do we get rid of this giant?! It is for this purpose the story is preserved.

LAHMI, THE PHILISTINE

Here we have a giant that should send shivers down our spine!

Lahmi is another Philistine champion. Again, we face the enemy of all good in one of its most powerful forms. The battle with this giant is a direct confrontation with humanistic philosophy, with worldliness in a most alluring and attractive guise. This was a giant the prince of Israel could not fight. He had sinned. It had to be fought for him.

Lahmi's name means "foodful" or full of food. His intent is not just to kill and abandon, but rather to eat away at his victim until it is completely spent or devoured. Do you have anything that is "eating away" at your life forces or relationships, or draining your physical, mental, spiritual, social, or financial reserves from the inside out? You could be doing battle with Lahmi!

And he is not a giant to take lightly. His destructive force was compared to that of Goliath. In fact, this giant was not classed as the other three (termed "sons of the giant"). Lahmi was called a "brother." The emphasis in the original language is on likeness or kindred spirit. A formidable foe, to be sure!

HIS WEAPON

The only association given to the destructive power of this giant is a spear staff like a "weaver's beam." This is a curious comparison, for we don't usually consider "weavers" as being an intimidating lot or "weaver's beams" as being dangerous or life-threatening. There was something about the giant's spear shaft that caught the writer's attention, something that was frightening … or attractive. Why this association? And why omit the penetrating part of the spear—the spearhead?

As we probe into the Hebrew phrase, "weaver's beam," we must keep in mind that we are thinking about the description of an enemy's weapon.

What about this association with weavers? As we look through the places "weaver" is used in the Old Testament, we note it is simply referring to the making of cloth, like as worn for clothing. However, there is an association of garments with character, righteousness, and salvation:

> **"He wears clothes of vengeance. He wraps himself with fury as a coat"** (Isa. 59:17, GW).

> **"I will greatly rejoice in Jehovah, my soul will be joyful in my God; for He has clothed me with the robes of salvation, He covered me with the robe of righteousness like a bridegroom adorns himself with ornaments, and like a bride adorns herself with her jewels"** (Isa. 61:10, MKJV).

> **"You have a few names even in Sardis who have not defiled their garments. And they will walk with Me in white, for they are worthy.**

> The one who overcomes, this one will be clothed in white clothing. And I will not blot out his name out of the Book of Life, but I will confess his name before My Father and before His angels" (Rev. 3:4–5, MKJV).

The one who makes the clothes, then, the weaver, should have some power over the life, shouldn't he? The connection of weaver's with life and death is suggested in the references below:

> "My days go swifter than a weaver's shuttle. They are spent without hope" (Job 7:6, GW).

King Hezekiah of Judah wrote this after he was sick and became well again:

> I thought that in the prime of my life I would go down to the gates of Sheol and be robbed of the rest of my life. I thought that I wouldn't see the LORD in this world. Even with all the people in the world, I thought I would never see another person. My life was over. You rolled it up like a shepherd's tent. You rolled up my life like a weaver. You cut me off from the loom. You ended my life in one day. (Isa. 38:10–12, GW)

The word beam is used nine times in the Old Testament but with four different Hebrew words.

- Once in Judges 16:14 it refers to a weaver's shuttle
- Once in 1 Kings 7:6 as an architectural structure (a "thick beam")
- Twice in 2 Kings 6:2, 5 as referring to a wooden rafter as used in a building
- Once as a supplied word in Habakkuk 2:11 with reference to a tree
- And four times in reference to a giant's spear shaft (1 Sam. 17:7; 2 Sam. 21:19; 1 Chron. 11:23; 20:5)

If the Hebrew writer wanted to give us the idea of a thick wooden structure to compare the shaft to, he could have used any of the other three Hebrew words, and one of them (the weaver's shuttle) would have fit well with the "weaver" part. But he didn't do this. The association, apparently, was not with a thick, straight section of wood.

"Beam" can refer to a "yoke" or the "framework of a loom," perhaps a supporting part of it. This would be in keeping with the Hebrew word "chosen" and would be a figure people of that day could relate to. Looms were common then. And people would know the approximate size of the shaft by comparison to a common household appliance. And this is a permissible interpretation, according to the Hebrew. The support part is very helpful in understanding the weapon, but the structural image of a framework has little value to us today who are far removed from such appliances (it is difficult to imagine a spear shaft being something like a loom's framework), especially if we are trying to use the story, inspired by God, for "**teaching, pointing out errors, correcting people, and training them for a life that has God's approval**" (2 Tim. 3:16, GW). It seems there should be a broader application than "the framework of a loom," an application that would help us understand the characteristics of this giant, his terrible weapon, and how he works to destroy.

There is another deep association with this Hebrew word that none of the other words have—an association with light: "to glisten; a lamp (i.e., the burner) or light (literally or figuratively)."[12] If the writer were merely trying to help us get a picture of the size or massiveness of the spear's shaft, why would he use a word that was ambiguous when there were other common words far more descriptive? Why would he pick a word that also had an association with support and light as well as a loom's framework? The Hebrew word is used no other place in the Bible. Could it be he was trying to bend our mind into a new concept? That somehow the spear's shaft seemed to "glisten" or "burn" in the sunlight? (Perhaps the shaft had a metallic or bronze covering.) To a people who were used to wooden implements of war, this would indeed be novel or fearsome! (Spears of laser light are used today in imaginative futuristic battles.)

How does the concept of support and light make this weapon so terrible? To the Hebrew, light has always been coupled with God, His Word, or His kingdom. Elijah on Mount Carmel is a case in point (lightning licking up the offering). The sun turning backwards several degrees for Hezekiah is another (1 Kings 18:37–38; Isa. 38:8). If an enemy is associated with light, especially having some control of it (the burner), then it would appear he has God on his side or is using divine precepts in his warfare! This could be very scary, especially for those who put their dependence on God and His Word for their defense. Almost nothing is beyond the power of Satan to deceive, if possible, the very elect (Matt. 24:24).

---

[12] Strong's Concordance number for "beam" is H4500. It is from another word (H5214) which means "A root probably identical with that of H5216, through the idea of the *gleam* of a fresh furrow." H5216 means "properly meaning to *glisten*; a *lamp* (that is, the burner) or *light* (literally or figuratively)."

"**For such men are false Apostles, workers of deceit, making themselves seem like Apostles of Christ. And it is no wonder; for even Satan himself is able to take the form of an angel of light**" (2 Cor. 11:13–14, BBE).

It appears, then, the "weaver's beam" is referring to some aspect of the giant's weaponry that has a strong association with life and death but also includes a unique, unexpected twist—an association with apparent goodness and righteousness as its basis of support.

WHY NO SPEARHEAD?

The presence of a spearhead would immediately put us on the defensive. Is this person friend or foe? Why is he approaching me with a weapon? But if there is no obvious emblem of destruction, we are disarmed. It's like a fearsome dog growling at us, but we notice, when he curls his lips, he has no teeth! Would we be as afraid? Lahmi's intent is to deceive us so he can get close to us. He definitely has teeth, but he isn't going to show them! And the idea of "a gentle giant" is enhanced by the reference in 2 Samuel 21:19 to Goliath being a Gittite (a treader of grapes). The association: grapes > wine > good times (the Entertainer!).

PUTTING IT ALL TOGETHER

We have a giant who identifies himself with truth and goodness. We hear smooth and comforting words of Scripture (Matt. 4:6). We see evidences of divine power attending him (Matt. 7:22). We are disarmed and let him get close to us. What he says sounds so right! So, we adopt his teachings or try his suggestions.

Then, slowly, imperceptibly, we notice a weakness, a sickness, a lack of power. Lahmi has been quietly weaving humanistic philosophy into our experience. We are being consumed from the inside by worldly concepts and principles that we thought were heavenly.

As we follow the development of the giant image in Nebuchadnezzar's image, we notice the third kingdom, Greece, is represented by BRASS. This is the only metal in the lineup of kingdoms that is made in the crucibles of man. It is not found in nature. The association the Bible gives to "brass," then, is "human involvement," something happening "on this earth" (in contrast with that taking place "in heaven" or solely by heavenly beings). This association does not necessarily imply a negative association but just the idea that the human element is involved. Note a couple descriptions of the glorified Christ, the God who became man to save us. In both descriptions, His feet (the part that touched the earth) were compared to fine brass.

"Then I lifted up mine eyes, and looked, and behold a certain man clothed in linen, whose loins were girded with fine gold of Uphaz: His body also was like the beryl, and his face as the appearance of lightning, and his eyes as lamps of fire, and his arms and his feet like in colour to polished brass, and the voice of his words like the voice of a multitude" (Dan. 10:5–6).

"And in the midst of the seven candlesticks one like unto the Son of man, clothed with a garment down to the foot, and girt about the paps with a golden girdle. His head and his hairs were white like wool, as white as snow; and his eyes were as a flame of fire; and his feet like unto fine brass, as if they burned in a furnace; and his voice as the sound of many waters" (Rev. 1:13–15).

But brass, like all things, can be defiled. And when it is, it represents the human factor without God's help (humanism). Most of Goliath's armament and weaponry were associated with brass (human involvement).

"And there went out a champion out of the camp of the Philistines, named Goliath, of Gath, whose height was six cubits and a span. And he had an helmet of brass upon his head, and he was armed with a coat of mail; and the weight of the coat was five thousand shekels of brass. And he had greaves of brass upon his legs, and a target of brass between his shoulders" (1 Sam. 17:4–6).

We can see an example of this today in the influence of Greek philosophy in education and medicine. Greece, the kingdom of brass, is the model of humanistic philosophy. The whole world, it seems, has patterned their schools and practice of the healing arts after this humanistic model. Emulation, the scientific method in reasoning (exclusive of biblical interpretations), worldly philosophy, and other "contributions" the kingdom of "brass" has handed down, have had almost no objection from the Christian segment.

We can see what constitutes true "higher education" in the Savior's parable teaching. Christ said nothing to gratify curiosity or to satisfy ambition for worldly greatness.

We understand Jesus did not attend the schools of His day. God had a different plan of education than the popular Greek/Roman method then used. But we continue to use the Greek pattern for education: self-worship (love of praise enhanced by degrees and earning high "grades"), specializing (learning much about one field without seeing how it integrates with others), linear thinking (all learning leads man to feel more in control of his universe and less dependent on God).

The education Jesus received, however, was shown to be far superior, though He gained knowledge as we may do. We can see what constitutes true "higher education" in the Savior's parable teaching. Christ said nothing to gratify curiosity or to satisfy ambition for worldly greatness.

Today, however, we are confused. Our children are not learning as Christ learned. There is little difference between Christian schools and the best of the world's schools. (Do we not get "higher degrees" from the world and bring their knowledge back to our schools?) And the same can be said for the healing arts and agricultural methods. God's people have little advantage, if any, over the best the world offers. And we are all getting weaker and sicker. Our children use drugs like others, our marriages break up like others, our farmers work harder for less like others, our doctors are as impotent with the "incurables" as others. We have not yet discerned the cause. And we would continue so unless someone comes to our rescue, someone designed specifically to fight and destroy this terrible consuming giant in our life.

ELHANAN THE SON OF JAIR

As we look at Lahmi's antagonist, we shall first consider his home, then his father, then himself.

A Bethlehemite

His father, Jaareoregim, was a citizen of Bethlehem, as was the family of Jesse, King David's father, and the future birthplace of Jesus. The name of the town had the same Hebrew association as the giant Lahmi—bread, food, consume, devour—but with a slight difference. Bethlehem means "the house of bread" (house is associated with "family"). Where Lahmi represented the world's bread, Bethlehem directs us to the Bread of Life, the Savior, a member of the family of God. The bread Christ offers, draws us together in a kindred spirit. The bread of Lahmi draws us away from God and to self-seeking and hypocrisy. This is inherent in Christ's warning to "beware of the leaven of the Pharisees, and of the leaven of Herod" (Mark 8:15). See Luke 12:1.

Jaareoregim

His name is interpreted as "woods of weavers." Again, we have a parallel with the Philistine giant (weavers). Instead of a weaver's "beam" we have an association with a "forest"—a large gathering—of weavers. Where a single weaver is used to describe Lahmi, Jaareoregim represents a cluster of them. There is strength in numbers, in family, in unity and brotherhood.

Two are better than one; because they have a good reward for their labor. For if they fall, the one will lift up his fellow; but woe to him who is alone when he falls, for he does not have another to help him. Again, if two lie together, then they have warmth; but how can one be warm alone? And if one overthrows him, two shall withstand him; and a threefold cord is not quickly broken (Eccles. 4:9–12, MKJV)

"Without counsel purposes are disappointed: but in the multitude of counsellors they are established" (Prov. 15:22).

The son of Jaer

Elhanan was the son of Jaareoregim. He was "the builder of the family name" (as the Hebrews interpreted it). What Elhanan did would reflect on the whole character of his family. But to whatever his father signified in his name, Elhanan also adds his own unique qualities. He does not ignore his heritage but honors it and adds to it.

Elhanan

His name is composed of two Hebrew words: "El" and "Hanan."

The first, "El," is often used as a name for God, for it means "anything strong; specifically a chief (politically); also a ram (from his strength); a pilaster (as a strong support); an oak or other strong tree."[13]

We can see a tie-in to his family in this part of his name. Where his dad's name speaks of a copse of trees, Elhanan's name identifies the trees as oaks or other strong varieties. In other words, they are God-fearing leaders, upright Christians whose strength is in God, not man.

Up to this point, we have a picture of Lahmi's fearful adversary: one who, like himself, is well-versed in truth and things needful to sustain life, is associated with the very fabric of character, and can influence one for life or death. But where the Philistine stands in the power of his humanistic might, his enemy stands in the power of the whole family of heaven. Where the world's champion is defined by size (physical superiority), God's champion is defined by the name of his God, El.

We have one more part of Elhanan's name and one final comparison. The most descriptive part of the Philistine giant was in a likeness to his "brother" Goliath—the spear's shaft like a weaver's beam. In fact, one of the two accounts of this battle (2 Sam. 21:19) didn't even give Lahmi's name (that's why we put it in brackets in the beginning quote). We noted

---

[13] See Strong's Commentary on "el" (H410).

the possibility of the "beam" referring to support and light, which is often associated with God and the kingdom of heaven. The giant, however, uses a worldly counterfeit of this as a weapon to attack God's people and weaken and consume them. There was no notice of a spearhead, as Goliath had.

That which best describes Elhanan's success is in the last part of his name, HANAN, which means "gracious," "merciful." Though all the other parts of Elhanan's name and family and origin help in understanding how to do battle with Lahmi, this part is most critical. It is our dependence on the grace of God that victory is assured. Our confidence in His mercy and compassion on our weakness will tell whether we come out winner or loser in the fray. It is this that separates us from humanistic influences.

> *It was not Noah's faithfulness alone that saved his family and himself those fearful days and weeks. It was the grace and mercy of God! This is one of the most significant parts of Jehovah's character that He wishes us to keep in mind.*

When the world was overcome with sinners and God was about to wipe out the whole human race, He saw a single family that could be saved to repopulate the earth. To Noah He gave instructions how to build an ark that would save them from the coming tempest. Noah and his family followed the plan to the letter. Nothing was done that God did not approve, nor was anything omitted that God required. Everything was done to the letter. In the end, God was pleased and invited the family, and all those who would believe, into the ark. Then He closed the door and let the storm come.

It was not Noah's faithfulness alone that saved his family and himself those fearful days and weeks. It was the grace and mercy of God! This is one of the most significant parts of Jehovah's character that He wishes us to keep in mind. Remember when Moses asked to "see" Him? The Lord put him in a cleft of a rock and passed before him, declaring,

"I will make all My goodness pass before you, and I will proclaim the name of Jehovah before you. And I will be gracious to whom I will be gracious, and will have mercy on whom I will have mercy" (Exod. 33:19, MKJV).

"And Jehovah passed by before him and proclaimed, Jehovah! Jehovah God, merciful and gracious, long-suffering, and abundant in goodness and truth" (Exod. 34:6, MKJV).

When dissipation has replaced dedication, outgo exceeds income, health becomes a struggle, and cheerfulness a chore, then it may be more apparent that Lahmi, the champion of Philistine and Greek philosophies, has slipped into our camp and quietly feasted on our vitals while we played or slept. He has eaten the corn and left us the husk. The giant is a counterfeiter. The laughter he generates is a façade, a cloak to hide the pain of having our vitals slowly eaten away. We have found his breads are parasites. His sweets turn the belly sour. His good times leave remorse and emptiness. What are we to do?

In the name of the gracious God, Elhanan slew the devouring giant. And in the same name we can too!

- **Bethlehemite:** (house of bread) It is the Word of God, in its myriad forms, that is the true foundation and support for all thought and action. Seek those who love to feast on the Word. Pray with them. Study with them. Share with them. Work with them. They are family, and they are there to help us, and we them.

- **Jaareoregim:** (woods of weavers) Do not ignore those people and things that God uses to develop character, to beautify the life and lengthen it. But never depend on the counsel of just one. Go to others in similar work. Look for counsel and enlightenment among a host of God-fearing people, in His Word, in nature, in providential leadings. Forsake not the assembling of yourselves together (Heb. 10:25). Truth is always consistent with itself, no matter what form it may be in.

- **Elhanan:** (God is gracious) And when all this is done, cast your helpless soul on the mercies of God and the merits of His Son, then watch Him do His gracious (undeserving) work. Doing our part opens the door for Him to do His. It doesn't obligate Him to. He has wanted to all along. It just puts us in the proper attitude and position for Him to help. So, when He does, we know whom to praise.

And with all that working for us, the Entertainer doesn't have the last laugh!

Chapter 4

THE INTERPRETER

*"And there was yet a battle in Gath,
where was a man of* **great** *stature,
that had on every hand six fingers, and on every foot six toes,
four and twenty in number;
and he also was born to the giant.
And when he defied Israel,
Jonathan the son of Shimea
the brother of David
slew him."*
2 Samuel 21:20–21

The Interpreter is a different breed. He doesn't stand before imposing audiences when he does his thing, nor is he there for the daily grind. He does his work quietly, purposefully, building slowly ... but strong.

- It may be a mother holding a spoon with a new food in front of her little infant, and smiling, saying, "Open wide, honey. This will help you grow big and strong."
- It might be a first-grade teacher interpreting interesting shapes as numbers or letters or words upon which the children's whole educational life will be built.
- It might be a doctor looking over some lab test results and pointing to some numbers with "HIGH" OR "LOW" before them and saying, "This is why you aren't feeling well." He then prescribes a "get well" program and sends his patient home.

These (and many more can be given) are illustrations of how dependent we are on the Interpreters in our life. Their influence is powerful, for what we are taught in our innocence can go with us the rest of our life, molding our thoughts, choices, arguments, and behavior. And this will be whether the Interpreter is Jesus decoding the principles of heaven during His sermon on the mount, or a talking serpent handing us a fruit from the tree of knowledge and explaining how it will make us stronger and wiser—and all based upon observable "facts."

This interpreter is perceived as an enemy of God's kingdom. However, one thing that seems to enhance an interpreter's influence is when he is cloaked in mystery, and that is certainly the case with this giant. The more mystical, the more powerful.

By now it has been quite apparent that each giant studied has been a counterpart of one of the kingdoms of Nebuchadnezzar's image described in Daniel 2. This giant is no exception. The description in the verse above identifies him with the iron kingdom, specifically, the notable horn of Rome.

1. no name given
2. the place of battle
3. size
4. association with a number
5. his father
6. the circumstances of his death

1. NO NAME GIVEN

This fourth giant in our study remains nameless, though his three brothers were identified by names—just like the fourth kingdom in Daniel 7 (the first three were described as specific creatures; the fourth was not identified with any particular animal):

"**The first** *was* **like a lion**" (Dan. 7:4, NKJV).

"**And behold another beast, a second, like to a bear**" (Dan. 7:5).

"**After this I beheld, and lo another, like a leopard**" (Dan. 7:6)

"**After this I saw in the night visions, and behold a fourth beast, dreadful and terrible, and strong exceedingly**" (Dan. 7:7).

Names often describe origin or identify specific characteristics.

"**And Adam said, This is now bone of my bones, and flesh of my flesh: she shall be called Woman, because she was taken out of Man**" (Gen. 2:23).

"And the angel of the LORD said unto her, Behold, thou *art* with child and shalt bear a son, and shalt call his name Ishmael [God will hear]; because the LORD hath heard thy affliction" (Gen. 16:11).

"Therefore the Lord himself shall give you a sign; Behold, a virgin shall conceive, and bear a son, and shall call his name Immanuel [God is with us]" (Isa. 7:14).

If a name is purposely withheld in describing an individual, then something of a mystery surrounds that person, AT LEAST AS FAR AS UNDERSTANDING HIM. Who is he? Where does he come from? What is his purpose for being here? What is he really like? Such a mystery encircles the horn of Rome who is out to take God's place.

"**Let no man deceive you by any means: for that day shall not come, except there come a falling away first, and that man of sin be revealed, the son of perdition; Who opposeth and exalteth himself above all that is called God, or that is worshipped; so that he as God sitteth in the temple of God, shewing himself that he is God**" (2 Thess. 2:3–4).

In order to deceive, he must maintain an aura of mystery, so as not to be discovered. Is he a serpent (Gen. 3:1)? Is he an "angel of light" (2 Cor. 11:14)? Is he a lion (1 Peter 5:8)? When Jesus was about to help a man vexed with a power of darkness, He demanded the devil to identify himself by name.

"**And Jesus asked him, saying, What is thy name? And he said, Legion: because many devils were entered into him**" (Luke 8:30).

2. THE PLACE OF BATTLE

It's not very difficult to portray certain characteristics on a person when you know something about the place of battle—especially if that person is there voluntarily and leading the fray. Consider these individuals: [a] a religious zealot, [b] an anti-abortion advocate, [c] a power-hungry world leader, [d] a racial extremist, and [e] a powerful labor union activist. In what battle would you place each in the list that follows? Would you expect to find them in one or more of the other activities?[14]

    1. A country with rich oil fields

    2. A recently burned abortion center

    3. A large nonunionized assembly plant

    4. An isolated religious community in Waco, Texas

    5. A white segregated bus in which a black woman demands a ride

---

[14] Answer key: a-4, b-2, c-1, d-5, e-3.

How did you do? Was it hard to match them up? It works the same way with this giant. The only time we hear of him is when he is trying to defend or capture Gath. Obviously, there is something about Gath that interests him.

Gath was likely home territory since it was the home of Goliath (1 Sam. 17:4, 23), this giant's deceased father. It occupied a strong position on the borders of Judah and Philistia. It had been one of the royal cities of the Philistines, but was at this time now part of Canaan, the inheritance of God's people. As we follow the history of Gath throughout the Old Testament, we notice it is constantly being captured and recaptured. It appears in 1 Chronicles 18:1 that David conquered the city, yet we find in 1 Chronicles 20:6 that the Philistines, led by this giant, had initiated another battle here. There is something about Gath that appears very important to both camps. Perhaps the name may help us a bit.

The name "Gath" means "wine vat," a place for holding grapes in pressing them. Grapes, wine, vineyards, besides offering valuable industries, have often had spiritual associations.

"**For the vineyard of the LORD of hosts is the house of Israel**" (Isa. 5:7).

"**Hear another parable: There was a certain householder, which planted a vineyard, and hedged it round about, and digged a winepress in it, and built a tower, and let it out to husbandmen, and went into a far country .... And when the chief priests and Pharisees had heard his parables, they perceived that he spake of them** [the husbandmen of the vineyard]" (Matt. 21:33, 45).

"**This cup** [of grape juice] **is the new testament in my blood, which is shed for you**" (Luke 22:20).

"**And another angel came out from the altar, which had power over fire; and cried with a loud cry to him that had the sharp sickle, saying, Thrust in thy sharp sickle, and gather the clusters of the vine of the earth; for her grapes are fully ripe**" (Rev. 14:18).

The association of the giant with "wine vats" suggests this giant may have some connection with spiritual powers. As we look at the little horn power, the haughty see of Rome, we notice he, too, is connected with grapes and wine.

"**With whom the kings of the earth have committed fornication, and the inhabitants of the earth have been made drunk with the wine of her fornication**" (Rev. 17:2).

The woman of Revelation 17, representing Babylon, is described as "arrayed in purple and scarlet colour, and decked with gold and precious stones and pearls, having a golden cup in her hand full of abominations and filthiness" (Rev. 17:4). She represents a church, a persecuting power, "drunken with the blood of the saints" (Rev. 17:6). This power was the church of Rome who for centuries persecuted and killed Christians who didn't follow her dogmas.

3. SIZE

A point is made of the giant's size. Height is often equated with greatness in figurative language. The taller a person, the more they are usually feared or respected. One of the names of God is "the most high God."[15] Apparently, this giant represents something **very important.** The Hebrew word used for "great stature" includes much more than physical height. It's a measurement word: tribute (as measured), a vesture or dress (as measured), a portion (as measured). Measurement, however, necessitates a standard, yet **we are not given an exact measurement, or a specific standard by which to measure this giant** (like cubits). It is left to us to use our own standard for "greatness." Also, the Hebrew word is associated with **extensiveness** (*as by stretching*). This suggests that the size may not **always be** actual, but occasionally inflated or stretched beyond normal limits, like a rubber band or balloon at its maximum.

Situations can make this giant appear larger than life—a significant characteristic of the little horn power of Rome. Much of her religion includes things to charm the eye and captivate the ear, to impress the senses of her greatness. Her grand cathedrals, lofty domes, pillared isles, unsurpassed music, imposing processions, jeweled shrines, exquisite sculptures, captivating artistry, and colorful robes appeal to the senses but do not necessarily give evidence of a pure heart.

"Woe unto you, scribes and Pharisees, hypocrites! for ye are like unto whited sepulchres, which indeed appear beautiful outward, but are within full of dead men's bones, and of all uncleanness. Even so ye also outwardly appear righteous unto men, but within ye are full of hypocrisy and iniquity" (Matt. 23:27–28).

Delicate refinement, lofty concepts of art, brilliancy of style are not necessarily an index of holy, elevated thought. They often exist in minds that are sensual and worldly. Satan can use these to lead people to forget the necessities of the soul, to focus on the earthly attractions instead of the future, immortal life, to turn away from their infinite Helper, and to live for this world alone. A religion based on externals is attractive to the unconverted heart. Pomp and ceremony can have a seductive, bewitching

---

[15] Daniel 5:18; Mark 5:7.

power to such a soul; and they come to look upon the Roman church as the very gate of heaven.

In God's kingdom, true wealth is measured on the inside.

"But the LORD said unto Samuel, Look not on his countenance, or on the height of his stature; because I have refused him: for the LORD seeth not as man seeth; for man looketh on the outward appearance, but the LORD looketh on the heart" (1 Sam. 16:7).

God does not make the outside appear more important (or even equal in value) than what is on the inside. In the sanctuary that the Lord directed Moses to build, imposing and grand architecture was omitted. There was nothing on the outside to attract the senses. This was to be an illustration of Himself,[16] when He would come as a man.

> *In God's kingdom, true wealth is measured on the inside.*

"For he shall grow up before him as a tender plant, and as a root out of a dry ground: he hath no form nor comeliness; and when we shall see him, there is no beauty that we should desire him" (Isa. 53:2).

This giant is considered VERY IMPORTANT, yet no standard is given to define his actual size. In fact, it is even suggested his size could be stretched or inflated. This indicates our perception of him as an enemy may be dependent on things not all related to real size or worth. <u>This, the Bible is telling us, will characterize the little horn power of Rome.</u>

4. ASSOCIATION WITH A NUMBER

We must ever keep in mind that our introductory text is describing an <u>enemy</u>, and in this case, we are to fear more **who or what he is** than any physical weapon he may try to use against us.

So, we are now instructed to look at his hands and feet. What do they tell us?

Look what the Bible associates the **hands** with—the things we do for others or ourselves.

"Whatever your hand finds to do, do it with all your might; for there is no work, nor plan, nor knowledge, nor wisdom, in the grave where you go" (Eccles. 9:10, MKJV).

Hands can also express <u>thought</u>, like in sign language. Have you ever watched a person making gestures with his hands while talking on a phone?

---

[16] "But He spake of the temple of His body" (John 2:21).

It's just part of our nature to "talk" with our hands! Hands are used for so many things. Often, when we are grieving we wring our hands, or when feeling need of help we hold out our hands to others. It was a common practice to raise the hands in worship and praise. Hands are so much involved in the activities of mankind that often the hand alone is used to represent the person's thought. The mark of the beast, spoken about in Revelation 13:16, is given in the hand as well as in the forehead. The bloodless hand that wrote out Belshazzar's sentence (Dan. 5) expressed the thoughts of the Great Judge Himself.

Hands identify with service as well. Without hands, helping others would become most difficult.

Feet are associated with the choices we make (Ps. 73:2), or the direction we take in life (Ps. 119:105; Eph. 6:15). To try to help His disciples understand the true nature of their hearts, Christ washed their feet. Mary Magdalene, wanting to express her love and devotion before His death, anointed Jesus' feet (as well as His head) with a costly ointment.

If you strip everything mankind does as represented by the hands and feet, you have very little left, except perhaps for some intellectual concepts! It is interesting that both Christ's hands and feet were impaled to the cross, as if everything He tried to do for His people and the principles He stood for were rejected. These four members (two hands and two feet) represent **the expression of man's thought and actions**. The only other way he can express himself is with his head, and we shall be considering that shortly (but it won't be any different than what he does with his hands and feet!).

As we look at this giant's external members, we are considering his *real* nature, what he *does*, and where he is heading in *life*. And we see something very unusual. He has six fingers on each hand and six toes on each foot. The Scripture makes quite a point of this, even giving the total number of digits (twenty-four) that we not misunderstand.

What this does is gets us to think that the number six with this particular enemy is not normal. Every place we expect to see five, we see six. Something has been added, and because we are considering an enemy, that something is NOT GOOD!

THE ADDITION OF 1 [one]

In Hebrew, the number six is considered simply as an overplus (beyond the five fingers of the hand). But what the addition of one does in the story is noteworthy.

1) It draws attention to the giant's hands (works) and feet (ways).

2) It links these with an abnormality, something out of the ordinary.

3) It associates the number six with an enemy of God's people.

This association is also made with the giant's counterpart, the little horn power, in Revelation.

"**Here is wisdom. Let him that hath understanding count the number of the beast: for it is the number of a man; and his number is six hundred three score and six**" (Rev. 13:18).

Note this is an addition to God's plan, not a substitution—something added to what God has created. Why this extra digit on each hand and foot? Is this an indication of special favors … or powers?

THE UNFAVORABLE ELEMENT

Since the unnamed giant is portrayed as an enemy of God's people, the variation in number that describes him must contain an unfavorable element, something unique that is not available to those who are "confined" to five. Whenever man tries to improve on God's creations, all he can do is degrade them. Genetic modification is a current example. Though it may appear to benefit the plant kingdom for a while, it is doing havoc to the animal kingdom that feeds on it. And because the distortion is evident only in the feet and hands, we should see something added that affects the work of our hands and the direction given to our feet. This is similar to what free radicals do to healthy cells and tissues in the body. They add an **extra** element to normal cells and tissues, thus converting them to a toxic substance in the body.

The first we hear of an interpreter who adds to God's Word is very early in the biblical record, the third chapter of Genesis. However, this is not a fearful, terrible beast, but rather a dazzling (and charming) serpent in a tree. What was added to this creature that was not normal or expected? The gift of speech. And it claims it got this ability from eating from a tree God had forbidden. This is our next clue to this giant's character. The extra digit on each hand and foot should raise a big warning flag, but for the unsuspecting, it only raises a dangerous curiosity.

Let's first consider the normal, the five digits assigned to man on each hand and foot. What significance does the number five carry for what our hands do and where our feet carry us to? Using the Bible, we again find ourselves in Genesis, but this time in the very first chapter, considering what God did on the fifth day. As we look at Creation Week, we notice each day is characterized by something unique, some new dimension.

1. Light ... to make visible those things darkness hid from view
2. Firmament ... a livable space
3. Life ... in its most elementary form (plants)
4. 2 Great powers ... to rule the day and night
5. ?

As we look carefully at verses 20–21, we see a defining characteristic from the life forms created on day three, not just the creation of fish and fowl.

"**And God said, Let the waters bring forth abundantly** *the moving creature* **that hath life, and fowl** *that may fly* **above the earth in the open firmament of heaven. And God created great whales, and every living creature** *that moveth,* **which the waters brought forth abundantly, after their kind, and every winged fowl after his kind: and God saw that** *it was* **good**" (Gen. 1:20–21).

The moving creature (H8318). The emphasis here is on movement, active movement (voluntary), not passive (moving only because an outside force causes it—like wind blowing the leaves on a tree).[17]

That may fly (H5774). A new dimension of movement is added.[18]

That moveth (H7430)—to glide, crawl, or move with short steps. Here Moses uses another Hebrew word to highlight more types of movement.[19]

With these three Hebrew words, many types of movement are added to life forms (wiggling, creeping, crawling, gliding, walking, flying), but all have the capacity of voluntary movement, which plants do not have. These new life forms are FREE TO GO WHERE THEY WISH. Plants don't have that capacity. This characteristic of the number five carries all the way through the Bible. Other characteristics may be added to it, but never to negate this first capacity: freedom to move as we choose.

When we apply this to our hands and feet, it underscores the freedom to use them to do good or evil, to go heavenward or earthward: our own choice. We call that FREEDOM OF CHOICE—a freedom God's Son was willing to die to preserve, for our sakes. True education trains our hands in God-glorifying service and directs our feet to worthy destinations. But it

---

[17] Strong's on H8318: From H8317; a *swarm*, that is, active mass of minute animals: creep (-ing thing), move (-ing creature).
[18] Strong's on H5774: A primitive root; to *cover* (with wings or obscurity); hence (as denominative from H5775) to *fly*.
[19] Strong's on H7431: From H7430; a *reptile* or any other rapidly moving animal: - that creepeth, creeping (moving) thing. Strong's on H7430: A primitive root; properly to *glide* swiftly, that is, to *crawl* or *move* with short steps; by analogy to *swarm*.

also addresses a fifth point, our head (that includes our five senses) so we can make good decisions.

This idea, about teachers represented by the head, hands, and feet, is brought out by Jezebel's death. That she was considered a teacher is supported in Revelation 2:20.

"**Notwithstanding I have a few things against thee, because thou sufferest that woman Jezebel, which calleth herself a prophetess, to teach and to seduce my servants to commit fornication, and to eat things sacrificed unto idols.**"

> *True education trains our hands in God-glorifying service and directs our feet to worthy destinations.*

So, King Ahab's wife, Jezebel, who commanded 450 prophets (teachers) of Baal, was used to seduce God's people. When her reign came to an end, notice what happened.

And as Jehu entered in at the gate, she said, Had Zimri peace, who slew his master? And he lifted up his face to the window, and said, Who is on my side? who? And there looked out to him two or three eunuchs. And he said, Throw her down. So they threw her down: and some of her blood was sprinkled on the wall, and on the horses: and he trode her under foot. And when he was come in, he did eat and drink, and said, Go, see now this cursed woman, and bury her: for she is a king's daughter. And they went to bury her: but they found no more of her than the skull, and the feet, and the palms of her hands. (2 Kings 9:31–35)

So it is with this giant. We see a deformity in what is taught. It is not to preserve our FREEDOM OF CHOICE but rather to enslave us. He does not support true education. He doesn't have that capacity. He is overtaken by another (serpent) power and is used to also enslave us as he has been enslaved. Just like the serpent Satan used at the tree was cursed by God. And this Philistine giant will do it by deception, by using false interpretations. And the more we entertain him, the more we give him liberty to change us into his image.

5. THE SON WHO DEFIES

It is implied in the giant's description that his father was Goliath. Like his brother, Lahmi, this giant also reflects an attribute of his father. Note what

Goliath did to arouse David's purpose to slay him, and what Goliath's unnamed son did to arouse David's nephew to kill him.

[About Goliath:] "**Your servant killed both the lion and the bear. And this uncircumcised Philistine shall be like one of them, since he has <u>defied</u> the armies of the living God**" (1 Sam. 17:36, MKJV).

[About the unnamed giant:] "**But when he <u>defied</u> Israel, Jonathan the son of Shimea David's brother slew him**" (1 Chron. 20:7).

The word "defied" means to defame.[20] Whatever he did, whatever he said, was an offense to God and an embarrassment to God's people. Both father and son were skilled in it.

If the father and son were so close, what effect would it have on the son to have his father killed by someone? To an unconverted heart, would **revenge** and bitterness be added to one's already evil character? Would it make him any more sly and cautious? This giant is downright dangerous! He reminds us of another giant we are warned about in the New Testament. He, too, is vengeful and bitter and very crafty!

"**Woe to the inhabitants of the earth and in the sea! For the Devil came down to you, having great wrath, knowing that he has but a little time**" (Rev. 12:12).

And he is likened to a serpent! (And note what the serpent does!)

"**And the great dragon was cast out, the old serpent called Devil, and Satan, who <u>deceives</u> the whole world. He was cast out into the earth, and his angels were cast out with him**" (Rev. 12:9, MKJV).

6. THE BATTLE

"**And when he defied Israel, Jonathan the son of Shimeah, the brother of David, killed him**" *(*2 Samuel 21:21, MKJV).

Nothing happened until the giant opened his mouth. Deception is a terrible thing. It is designed to be transparent, silent, tasteless, odorless, and even somewhat pleasurable. It can be all around us and within us with everything appearing normal. And if we're around it long enough, we will eventually invite it into our schools to teach our children, look for it in our healthcare facilities to get us well, and insist on its smooth words in the pulpits to direct our worship. During the day we will run our businesses and factories by it and seek for it to entertain us in the evening. All is well, until Deception opens its mouth.

---

[20] Strong's on H2778: A primitive root; to *pull* off, that is (by implication) to *expose* (as by *stripping*); specifically to *betroth* (as if a surrender); figuratively to carp at, that is, *defame*.

And what comes out? The very spirit that inspired it: bitterness, hatred, blasphemies, belittling accusations, faultfinding, defiance, resentments, and curses. Often Satan deceives us to divert our loyalty to him, and then humiliates and embarrasses us by that very loyalty, causing guilt and shame. Deception makes no friends. It's a fiendish foe that enjoys belittling its victims until there is no joy left in life. When Deception finally speaks, we realize we have been duped and are powerless against it. Some who have heard its voice have ended their life to silence their torment. Others turn to vice after vice to drown out those voices. Still others mysteriously lose their minds or go on a killing rampage on those around them. Very few turn to God.

This defiance of God and His believers is another characteristic of the beast of Rome (Dan. 7:8; Rev. 13:5).

God is our only answer. He knows who to send to help us, as He did for the sin-weakened king of Israel— sending David's nephew, his third oldest brother's son. We'll look soon at the deliverer God designed to destroy this most terrible giant.

KINGDOM OF IRON

You may have observed with the other three giants a comparison has been made with the first three kingdoms of Daniel 2, **in order**. It would be hard to miss it.

Babylon—gold—self-sufficient prosperity
Medo-Persia—silver—obedience to human laws—limiting
Greece—brass—worldly philosophy, humanism—consuming

You may have also noted that God's solutions to each of the problems included His version of the main theme.

- The slayer of Ishbibenob, Worldly Prosperity, was one who used prosperity to help those suffering and in need. Both were identified by the prosperous number 300.

- Saph, the great Coach, fell at the hand of him who learned to limit his counselors and friends to those who were full of faith and enthusiasm for the advancement of God's kingdom.

- Lahmi, the Philistine champion who used worldly philosophy to corrupt divine truth and consume us from within, was overcome by God's champion who had Truth, the True Bread, as his counselor (as well as those who also depended on God for protection and guidance) and the graciousness of God as his defender.

Well, we have come to the fourth giant and the fourth kingdom. By now we should be thinking, "What can the iron kingdom of Rome teach me about this mysterious no-named giant?"

"**After this I saw in the night visions, and behold a fourth beast, dreadful and terrible, and strong exceedingly; and it had great iron teeth: it devoured and brake in pieces, and stamped the residue with the feet of it: and it *was* diverse from all the beasts that *were* before it; and it had ten horns**" (Dan. 7:7).

What does IRON characterize? And what did IRON symbolize in history? Simply put, it is <u>strength and force to the rulers</u>, the <u>loss of power of choice and independent action</u> to the subjects of the kingdom. In Christ's time, Rome was in power, and the Jews hated the Roman yoke. They longed to break its control over their nation and hoped Christ would be the promised deliverer. Well, He was, but not in the way they were hoping. Christ taught them to not resist the Roman yoke.

"**And whoever shall compel you to go a mile, go with him two**" (Matt. 5:41, MKJV).

> ***And whosoever shall compel thee to go a mile, go with him twain**—an allusion, probably, to the practice of the Romans and some Eastern nations, who, when government despatches had to be forwarded, obliged the people not only to furnish horses and carriages, but to give personal attendance, often at great inconvenience, when required. But the thing here demanded is a readiness to submit to unreasonable demands of whatever kind, rather than raise quarrels, with all the evils resulting from them. What follows is a beautiful extension of this precept.*[21]

Brutal force is often characteristic of weakness.

"**Paul now returned to Damascus, and preached boldly in the name of Jesus. The Jews could not withstand the wisdom of his arguments, and they therefore counseled together to silence his voice by force—the only argument left to a sinking cause. They decided to assassinate him.**"[22]

The unnamed foe of God's people is not just an imp who enjoys tricking us any chance he can get for a good laugh but an evil mind that wants **complete control of us**, and then to spit us out onto the rubbish heap when he is through with us. He accomplishes his end by DISTORTING

---

[21] D.D. Robert Jamieson, A.R. Fausset and David Brown, "Commentary Critical and Explanatory on the Whole Bible," Study Light, https://1ref.us/1se (accessed November 17, 2021).

[22] Ellen G. White, *The Spirit of Prophecy* (Battle Creek, MI: Seventh-day Adventist Publishing Association, 1878), p. 319, emphasis mine.

OUR DISCERNING POWERS so he can force us into doing those things we would be aghast to do were we in our right mind. The intent of this kind of deception is to bind us by iron chains to obedience to Satan's dictates. Daniel 2 tells us that the kingdom of iron extends all the way to the time of the end (represented by the feet). This unnamed giant is a last-day issue as well.

If this giant is anything like his brothers, then we should expect his demise would involve a different kind of force, and a different kind of obedience, a divine application of "iron" in the very end of time. A brief look in Revelation shows that we shall not be disappointed!

And "He will shepherd them with an iron staff" (they are "broken to pieces like clay vessels"), as I also have received from My Father" (Rev. 2:27, LITV).

"And she bore a son, a male, who is going to rule all nations with a rod of iron. And her child was caught up to God and to His throne" (Rev. 12:5, MKJV).

"And out of His mouth goes a sharp sword, so that with it He should strike the nations. And He will shepherd them[23] **with a rod of iron. And He treads the winepress of the wine of the anger and of the wrath of Almighty God"** (Rev. 19:15, MKJV). [Is there a connection here with winepress (Gath) and iron?]

God's Deliverer: JONATHAN = JEHOVAH-GIVEN

God has many names in the Bible. What is special about this name, Jehovah, the I AM, the Self-Existent One, that helps define the one who slew this giant? The name comes from the root "to be or become." Jehovah points to <u>Himself</u> becoming the Child of Bethlehem, One (become) <u>like us</u>. God first made man in His perfect image, then He made Himself into our fallen image. What love!

"It was Christ who from the bush on Mount Horeb spoke to Moses saying, 'I AM THAT I AM: Thus shalt thou say unto the children of Israel, I AM hath sent me unto you.' This was the pledge of Israel's deliverance. So when He came 'in the likeness of men,' He declared Himself the I AM. The Child of Bethlehem, the meek and lowly Saviour, is God 'manifest in the flesh.' 1 Timothy 3:16."[24]

It connects Christ to us as our Savior, the One we are to behold, that we may become <u>like Him</u> in character (the **object** of true education).

---

[23] [lead them to green pastures]
[24] Ellen G. White, *The Faith I Live By* (Washington, DC: Review and Herald, 1958), p. 47, emphasis mine.

The incarnate I AM is our abiding Sacrifice. The I AM is our Redeemer, our Substitute, our Surety. He is the Daysman between God and the human soul, our Advocate in the courts of heaven, our unwearying Intercessor, pleading in our behalf His merits and His atoning sacrifice. The I AM is our Saviour. In Him our hopes of eternal life are centered. He is an ever-present help in time of trouble. In Him is the assurance of every promise. We must acknowledge and receive this almighty Saviour; we must behold Him, that we may be like Him in character. "As many as received Him, to them gave He power to become the sons of God, even to them that believe on His name."[25]

It leads us to the third angel's message, the message that presents the character of Christ to a fallen world (the work of true education).

"The truths of the third angel's message have been presented by some as a dry theory; but in this message is to be presented Christ the Living One. He is to be revealed as the first and the last, as the I AM, the Root and the Offspring of David, and the bright and morning Star. Through this message the character of God in Christ is to be manifested to the world."[26]

What about the—GIVEN[27] part of his name? It was not a reward for some heroic deed nor a wage for faithful service. This Babe of Bethlehem was God's all-sufficient **gift** to us, an undeserved gift that satisfies all of our needs. God foresaw our condition and gave us what would satisfy our need, that nothing would hinder us in our return to Him. The intent of this gift was not to force us back into His presence with mindless obedience but to open pathways whereby we could voluntarily choose His presence again. It dispels the darkness of deception. But the gift can become that which finally condemns us.

The son of Shimeah: he that is heard and obeyed

Shimeah was a brother of David, the third oldest brother. The root meaning of his name means "He that is heard, he that is obeyed."[28] Shimeah was present when Goliath defied the armies of Israel, but he did nothing. He

---

[25] Ellen G. White, "The Word Made Flesh," *The Signs of the Times*, May 3, 1899, emphasis mine.
[26] Ellen G. White, *Testimonies for the Church, vol. 6* (Mountain View, CA: Pacific Press, 1901), p. 20, emphasis mine.
[27] That is in reference to God's deliverer: Jonathan = Jehovah—Given. We addressed the Jehovah part, now we will address the Given part.
[28] H8093 Feminine of H8088; *annunciation* H8088 From H8085; something *heard*, that is, a *sound, rumor, announcement*; H8085 A primitive root; to *hear* intelligently (often with implication of attention, obedience, etc.).

was unfaithful to his name. He saw David take on the giant. What could have been his victory was conferred on his little brother.

> **Now David was the son of that Ephrathite of Bethlehem-judah named Jesse, who had eight sons; and he was an old man in Saul's day, and far on in years. And the three oldest sons of Jesse had gone with Saul to the fight: the names of the three who went to the fight were Eliab, the oldest, and Abinadab the second, and Shammah the third. And David was the youngest. And the three oldest followed Saul.** (1 Sam. 17:12–14, BBE)

No doubt David's example was not forgotten, along with the fact that God's messenger, Samuel, when looking to anoint the next king-to-be, had looked straight into Shimeah's eyes and said, "This is not the man" (1 Sam. 16:10, paraphrase). Whatever stories Shimeah told his sons must have included his brother's courage to face the giant in the name of Israel's God, and the triumph that followed. And I suspect that there must also have been a humble confession of his weakness and an encouragement to his sons to be strong for the Lord, and obedient to His Word. Whatever went on in those family counsels and evening chats, we do know a resolve was born in one of his sons, Jonathan, to be obedient to God's "still small voice" and not to be afraid.

THE THIRD SON

In Bible times, position in the birth-line was important. The first-born automatically was assigned a double portion of the inheritance. When a dream was given that one of Jacob's sons should have the others bow down to him, it would have been one thing to have it one of the eldest sons of the patriarch, but the eleventh son? Even the father, who loved Joseph immensely, had a hard time with that.

What about the third position? Was there any significance to that? Many interesting things have happened in the third position. [Note we are discussing three this time as a position in place of a quantity. It carries a different meaning.]

- The first time "third" is mentioned in the Bible is during the Creation Week. We notice that this is the first time a life form is created (plants—Gen. 1:12–13).
- The third son of Adam, Seth, born when Adam was 130 years old, was the one through whom the Redeemer (the life-giver) was to

come. When Seth was 105 years old, he had Enos. "Then began men to call upon the name of Jehovah" (Gen. 4:26, MKJV).

- The third river of Eden was called Hiddekel. It was by this river that Daniel received an important vision of the future (Dan. 10:4). It concerned what shall happen to God's (saved) people <u>in the latter days</u> (verse 14).
- The third use of "third" was in reference to the ark that <u>saved Noah</u> and his household. It mentioned a third story (Gen. 6:16).
- It was on the third day that Abraham received confirmation on where he was to offer his only son Isaac (Gen. 22:4).
- It was on the third day after receiving Joseph's interpretation of their dreams that the servants of Pharaoh—the butler and the baker—were given <u>judgment</u> (as Joseph said would happen) (Gen. 40:20–22).
- It was on the third month of leaving Egypt that the children of Israel came to Mt. Sinai, where they received God's <u>law</u> and began constructing the first <u>sanctuary</u> (Exod. 19:1).
- It was on the third day that Christ arose from the grave as the <u>life-giver</u> (Luke 24:46).

The list goes on and on. But a thread weaves through all the accounts, a thread of *life*, *salvation*, *judgment*—a fitting finale to a name of the third son of Jesse (which has in its roots "announcement, a wonderful thing"), wouldn't you say? Was this an intimation that somehow through his seed, life and judgment would come to Israel? At this point we can only surmise. It does fit. It's a thought we might want to keep in mind.

A LAST DAY BATTLE OF THE MIND

As we look at this mysterious unnamed giant, the reference to <u>true education</u> as the developer of man's potential, its threat by the number six, the element of <u>deception</u>, the loss of individuality through <u>force</u>, reference to last day scenarios, we wonder what the future holds.

> *America, ... where the greatest light from heaven has been shining upon the people, can become the place of greatest peril and darkness because <u>the people do not continue to practice the truth and walk in the light</u> .... The more nearly we approach the closing scenes of this earth's history, the more pronounced will be the work of Satan. Every species*

of DECEPTION will take the lead to divert the mind from God through Satan's devices.[29]

The only safety we have against the GIANT OF DECEPTION is faithful **obedience** to all that God has graciously given to us—given that we may know what His will is, as well as the grace sufficient to obey it. This is the essence of the third angel's message (another "third"—hmmm), to turn people's mind, heart, and soul back to God in faith and obedience, that they might have **life**. It is the last hope for mankind! And it is the only hope for true education to be restored to God's people, that they may make the advanced steps necessary for these last days. (My comments are in brackets.)

Jesus took upon Himself man's nature, that He might leave a pattern for humanity, complete, perfect. He proposes to make us like Himself, true in every purpose, feeling, and thought— true in heart, soul, and life. [This is true education!] *This is Christianity. Our fallen nature must be purified, ennobled, consecrated by obedience to the truth* [Shimeah]. *Christian faith will never harmonize with worldly* [Philistine] *principles; Christian integrity is opposed to all deception and pretense* [the sixth digit of the unnamed giant]. *The man who cherishes the most of Christ's love in the soul, who reflects the Saviour's image most perfectly* [as Jonathan reflected his father's image], *is in the sight of God the truest, most noble, most honorable man upon the earth* [and the greatest specimen of the purpose and goal of true education].[30]

APPEAL

Deception is not something that we can look inside and "see." It usually is transparent or hidden. It is not like Lahmi, where we can sense a "void" within, a weakness when we know we should be strong. It is not like Saph, with whom we have to battle daily to maintain an enthusiasm in the Lord's work. Nor is it like facing the very real allurements of Ishbibenob (prosperity). When deceived, we know it not. The only evidence is a smitten conscience when Deception opens its ugly mouth. And by then, for many, it is almost too late! What can we do, then?

"**But when he defied Israel,
   Jonathan** [Jehovah-given]

---

[29] Ellen G. White, *Selected Messages, book 3* (Washington, DC: Review and Herald, 1980), p. 387, emphasis mine.
[30] Ellen G. White, *Testimonies for the Church, vol. 5* (Mountain View, CA: Pacific Press, 1889), p. 235, emphasis mine.

the son of Shimeah [he who hears and does]
David's brother [positioned in God's family to bring life, salvation, and judgment]
slew him" (1 Chron. 20:7).

We come to **Jehovah-given** and humbly cast ourselves at His feet. We claim His promise of a new heart.[31] We search our hearts and pray David's prayer in Psalm 139.

"Search me, O God, and know my heart: try me, and know my thoughts: and see if there be any wicked way in me, and lead me in the way everlasting" (Ps. 139:23–24).

Then whatever God reveals to us, whatever we **hear**, let us, by His grace, **do it**! Those who don't understand may call it "legalism" or "works" or some other slandering word, but never mind them. Let us walk in the Light.

> *Deception is not something that we can look inside and "see." It usually is transparent or hidden.*

"My brethren, God calls upon you as His followers to walk in the light. You need to be alarmed. Sin is among us, and it is not seen to be exceedingly sinful. The senses of many are benumbed by the indulgence of appetite and by familiarity with sin. We need to advance nearer heaven."[32]

> We are now a strong people, if we will put our trust in the Lord; for we are handling the mighty truths of the word of God. We have everything to be thankful for. If we walk in the light as it shines upon us from the living oracles of God, we shall have large responsibilities, corresponding to the great light given us of God. We have many duties to perform, because we have been made the depositaries of sacred truth to be given to the world in all its beauty and glory. We are debtors to God to use every advantage He has entrusted to us to beautify the truth by holiness of character, and to send the messages of warning, and of comfort, of hope and love, to those who are in the darkness of error and sin.[33]

With a heart focused only on the goodness and glory of God, determined to renounce any idol He reveals and follow His leading, we are promised

---

[31] "A new heart also will I give you, and a new spirit will I put within you: and I will take away the stony heart out of your flesh, and I will give you an heart of flesh" (Ezek. 36:26).
[32] Ellen G. White, *The Adventist Home* (Hagerstown, MD: Review and Herald, 1952), p. 401, emphasis mine.
[33] Ellen G. White, *Christian Experience and Teachings of Ellen G. White* (Mountain View, CA: Pacific Press, 1922), p. 204, emphasis mine.

life, salvation, and *judgment.* The deceptive interpretations of the fourth beast do not need to affect us! The promise of TRUE EDUCATION is that the image of our Creator will be formed in us again, with the full potential for development and service intended, as in the beginning, and the world will see what the Lord can really do with a houseful of converted sinners!

Our only safety against being deceived is <u>faithful</u> <u>obedience</u> to God's Word. The darkness of deception will be replaced by the *Light of the world.*[34] True education, in its purest form, will be reinstated in God's church. The clear message of the kingdom of God will be given. And then the end will come (Matt. 24:14).

God, hasten that day!

---

[34] John 8:12.

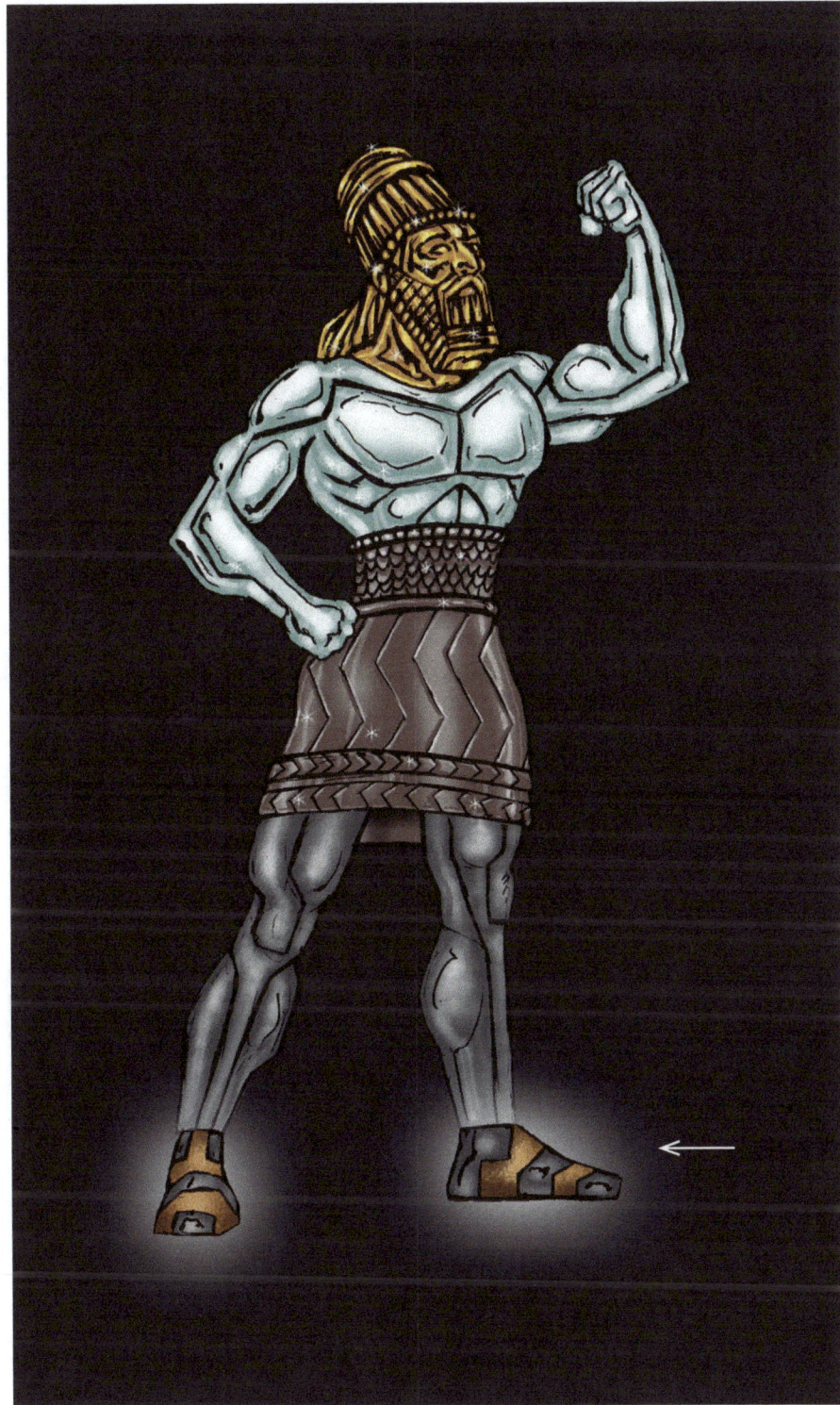

Chapter 5

THE FRIEND

*"And he slew an Egyptian,
a man of **great** stature [a goodly man],
five cubits high;
and in the Egyptian's hand was a spear like a weaver's beam;
and he went down to him with a staff,
and plucked the spear out of the Egyptian's hand,
and slew him with his own spear."*

1 Chronicles 11:23

Of all the associations we have, friends are usually considered the closest. Even to show the closeness of spouses, parents, and even God, if we also refer to them as our friends, nothing can get closer. Much is expected of friends that is not expected of any other relationship, because we are the most vulnerable around them, and they hold our most intimate secrets.

So, it is expected that to become our friend that person has to go through a probationary period beset with many rigorous trials and evaluations. But what happens when friends turn against us and betray us? Where or to whom can we turn? Well, that is what this last giant addresses. To many, it is the hardest form of deception we can endure. And, in fact, how sin began on this earth.

You will soon see we must, in the end, endure the same test Adam had in the beginning. His was not a deceptive serpent, but rather a deceived relative/neighbor/spouse—our dearest friends. But God has an answer for that too!

★ ★ ★ ★

A family is driving across the state, enjoying the rural scenery and having a good time, when a little child in the back seat says, "Wow! Did you see that horse? It was huge!" Now "huge" is not an exact word, so everyone wants to know what was meant by "huge." How do they find out? They ask the child if it was as tall as "that horse ahead of us?" "Taller!" he says with excitement. *Hmmm*. Need to look for something bigger. "How about that stand of field corn over there? It's about seven feet high by now," the dad says. "Oh, much taller than that!" the child exclaims. Now he has their attention. "How tall was the horse, son?" Mom asks. The child is quiet for a while, looking for something to compare to. Then, with obvious enthusiasm, his little finger begins jabbing the air at something near the road ahead of them, and he shrieks, "That tall! That tall! The horse was as tall as that!" Everyone follows his finger to a billboard a few hundred feet ahead. "Oooooh," they say. Guessing that it wasn't a real horse, they ask the little boy, "Was it a horse on the billboard?" "Yes!" he says with a satisfied smile. He finally got through.

We do a lot of comparison during the day. Someone says the watermelon was really sweet this time. "Was it as sweet as the one last week?" we ask. A commercial tries to sell a concentrated laundry soap. "One-fourth cup will do as much as one cup of your old powder," the salesman croons. "Mommy! Try this chair," a girl says while visiting a furniture store. "It's much softer than our old one." "These tires will last twice as long as those economy ones," the serviceman explains. Comparing one thing to another to help us understand it is very common, even in the Bible.

God tells us not to speak in an "unknown tongue" if there is no interpreter.

"If one speaks in a language, let it be by two, or at the most three, and in succession. And let one interpret. But if there is no interpreter, let him be silent In a church; and let him speak to himself and to God." (1 Cor. 14:27–28, MKJV).

If He tells us not to speak in a way others cannot understand, then He wouldn't do it Himself.

If He tells us not to speak in a way others cannot understand, then He wouldn't do it Himself. When God uses figurative language in the Bible, we can expect He provides the means by which we can interpret what is being said. Sometimes that which is provided to help us understand will lead us into unexpected fields, ones we may never have thought of before. Such is the power and challenge of comparative study. It takes work but is very rewarding.

> *In the Scriptures thousands of gems of truth lie hidden from the surface seeker. The mine of truth is never exhausted. The more you search the Scriptures with humble hearts, the greater will be your interest, and the more you will feel like exclaiming with Paul: "O the depth of the riches both of the wisdom and knowledge of God! how unsearchable are his judgments, and his ways past finding out!"*[35]

If the information is not close by, then we go to where it is. If it is not on the surface, easy to pick up and use, then we dig until we find it. The Interpreter is there! It's OK to compare and search. In fact, many stories are designed for this very purpose. This may require some effort, but it is that very effort that strengthens our minds!

> *The noble powers of the mind may be so dwarfed by lack of exercise on themes worthy of their concentration as to lose their ability to grasp the deep meaning of the word of God. The mind will enlarge if it is employed in tracing out the ... subjects of the Bible, comparing scripture with scripture, and spiritual things with spiritual. There is nothing more calculated to strengthen the intellect than the study of the Scriptures. No other book is so potent to elevate the thoughts, to give vigor to the faculties, as the broad, ennobling truths of the Bible. If God's word were studied as it should be, men would have a breadth of mind, a nobility of character, and a stability of purpose [that is] rarely seen in these times.*[36]

Like in this present study, we are trying to understand who or what this Egyptian giant represents. Because we are not told directly, we must go in search of an understanding. Several clues are given us. As we look at these clues, we seek for similar things to compare to or for an explanation from the original language.

THE LAST GIANT

The last giant is markedly different ... for good reason. He represents Satan's last-ditch effort to control the soul. Like the fourth giant, he is not named. Mystery also surrounds him. By using this fiend, the adversary pulls out all the stops, putting on his best façade, using his smoothest voice, and displaying his most convincing deceptions. Like clay which can

---

[35] Ellen G. White, *Maranatha* (Washington, DC: Review and Herald, 1976), p. 44, emphasis mine.
[36] Ellen G. White, *Steps to Christ* (Mountain View, CA: Pacific Press, 1892), p. 90, emphasis mine.

contain traces of all the elements, in this giant we can see elements of all the giants, and more.

A RECAP

We have been looking at an image of huge proportions, recorded as a single figure in Daniel 2. In it, God illustrated the diverse kingdoms that would rule the world. As we are discovering, these kingdoms did not just represent political powers. They also prefigured fearsome worldly influences to distract and deceive all of God's people, as made plain through the imagery of giants. Ignorance is lethal. They are no idle threats.

- Fortune: Satan's first effort to divert our allegiance to God is with the trappings of Babylon's prosperity. Prosperity and fortune are anything real or imagined that lifts us above our fellow man. Subtly and not so subtly, he tries to charm us to abandon heavenly riches for base worldly ones.

- Fears, Faults, and Failures: If the devil can't allure us away from true worship, he will try accusations, legal action, fears, imaginations, or some other way to LIMIT our service, as Medo-Persian princes tried to do with Daniel.

- Facts: Through worldly (Greek) education and philosophy, he tries to disarm those obedient to heaven's principles. He will reason with us in the guise of an educator or spiritual leader, to subtly change our thoughts via the most convincing arguments of tradition, worldly philosophy, or science. Just laugh and your problems will go away.

- Force: If Satan can't lure us into sin or limit our witness of God's goodness or "reason" with us through false sciences, then he purposes to force the faithful into submission. This force comes in many forms including embarrassment or humiliation, dishonor, physical pain or torture, and death threats. We saw this played out in the treatment of Christ when Rome was fairly new in power.

Satan's most convincing lies, his most subtle distortions are used to convince us to deny our heavenly heritage and leave the Lord's service. Yet in all these, God has His ways to deliver.

So, what is left? What other way can Satan try to break our union with Christ? It is his most powerful temptation; one he didn't even use on Christ in the wilderness. He saved it till the end. It is based on one of our most primitive needs: <u>Friendship</u>. The whole plan of redemption is relationship based. We are created as social beings. *"A friend in need is a friend indeed."* If you can't trust your friends, who can you trust? If you don't have friends, why try? The study on the Egyptian addresses this and how God will help.

The Bible presents this Egyptian as a giant, portrayed as Goliath and his "sons" were portrayed, in similar descriptive language, as though he represented similar dangers to God's people. We must understand the purpose of this comparison. To do so, we need first to comprehend the significance of clay.

THE CLAY

The whole image of Daniel 2 is a prophetic delineation of influences and powers that would affect God's people till the end of time. To think of them just as sovereign kingdoms ruling the world from Daniel's time to ours misses the intent of Scriptures. The Bible is not merely a book of history, politics, poetry, or prophecy. Its focus is not just "life on this earth". It is a divinely ordained collection of writings organized especially to instruct and inspire God's people throughout all ages, and lead them to their heavenly home, albeit through human failings, natural resources, political prowess, stories, parables, or a host of other means. He has power over all.

"All scripture is inspired by God and profitable for teaching, for reproof, for correction, and for training in righteousness" (2 Tim. 3:16, RSV).

We have been studying the four giants David did not (or could not) fight. We learned each had something in common. They were all Philistine sons of Goliath. We also learned how they compare to the characteristics of the Daniel 2 kingdoms, being listed in the same order as the kingdoms they represent. The world powers in Nebuchadnezzar's dream also shared a common factor. They were all represented by metals.

> *HOWEVER, AS DANIEL'S DESCRIPTION OF THE IMAGE DRAWS TO A CLOSE, SOMETHING UNIQUE SHOWS UP IN THE FEET. A NEW ELEMENT IS INTRODUCED BUT IT IS NOT A METAL, NOR DOES THE PROPHET TREAT IT AS A METAL. IT IS JUST COMMON CLAY. WHAT DOES THE CLAY REPRESENT?*

DUST/CLAY

The Bible's association with clay (or dust—in Hebrew *dust* can also be interpreted as clay, earth, mud) has often been with man—his mortality, his weakness and vulnerability, his utter inability to make of himself anything profitable without God's direct involvement.

"**And the LORD God formed man of the dust of the ground, and breathed into his nostrils the breath of life; and man became a living soul**" (Gen. 2:7).

"**For He knows our form; He remembers that we are dust**" (Ps. 103:14, MKJV).

"**All go to one place; all are of the dust, and all return to dust again**" (Eccles. 3:20, MKJV).

"**Does not the potter have power over the clay, from the same lump to make one vessel to honor and another to dishonor?**" (Rom. 9:21, MKJV).

Water dramatically affects clay but has little or no effect on gold, silver, brass, or iron. When water is mixed with clay, the clay is moldable, easily formed into many useful vessels. But remove the moisture and clay becomes hard, brittle, easily broken. How quickly we forget this. If God forms someone into a "vessel to honor" (ibid.) and then places him in His service, he may be tempted to think the gifts and graces given to fit him for service may be original with himself. What complicates matters is that sometimes God's gifts are permanent, even if one does not use them for His glory. It doesn't lessen the fact, however, that the gifts are still God's and we are only "earthen vessels" (2 Cor. 4:7), easily broken.

- Lucifer was created as the most exalted angel, actually next to Christ in glory and power. He took the glory to himself and became Satan, the life-destroyer and deceiver. Though now out of favor with God, he still retains much of his power. Even though he has been using it against God's government, he will eventually destroy himself with it.

- Moses was honed for a special work, to deliver God's people from the grip of Egypt. Part of that preparation was to have power over nature. Apparently, some of that which God did through him became his own. From then on, he could use that power for God's glory or his own. Unfortunately, he misused it once. When God commanded him to speak to a rock to have water come out, Moses, in a moment of passion, struck it instead with his rod, taking glory to himself. Water did come out, but the prophet was severely dealt with for misusing the gift (Num. 20:10–12).

- When God needed tradesmen to make the sanctuary, there were no Israelites skilled in the necessary crafts, so He poured His Spirit on two individuals, Bezeleel and Aholiab, immediately qualifying them for the task at hand. Once the sanctuary was completed these Israelites retained their skills, even passing them on to their children and grandchildren. ***"The descendants of these workmen inherited to a large degree the talents conferred on their forefathers."***[37] Solomon chose one of those descendants, Huram, of the line of Aholiab on his mother's side, to head up the construction of the new temple. Huram, even though inheriting many of Aholiab's skills, was himself unconverted. Read what effect his misuse had on the nation and Solomon himself.

Because of his unusual skill, Huram demanded large wages. Gradually the wrong principles that he cherished came to be accepted by his associates. As they labored with him day after day, they yielded to the inclination to compare his wages with their own, and they began to lose sight of the holy character of their work. The spirit of self-denial left them, and in its place came the spirit of covetousness. The result was a demand for higher wages, which was granted. The baleful influences thus set in operation permeated all branches of the Lord's service, and extended throughout the kingdom. The high wages demanded and received gave to many an opportunity to indulge in luxury and extravagance. The poor were oppressed by the rich; the spirit of self-sacrifice was well-nigh lost. In the far-reaching effects of these influences may be traced one of the principal causes of the terrible apostasy of him who once was numbered among the wisest of mortals.[38]

There are those, on the other hand, who remember their stewardship and consistently use their gifts for God's honor.

"The apostles and their associates were unlettered men, yet through the outpouring of the Spirit on the day of Pentecost, their speech, whether in their own or a foreign language, became pure, simple, and accurate, both in word and in accent."[39] *"From this time forth the language of the disciples was pure, simple, and accurate in word and accent, whether they spoke their native tongue or a foreign language."*[40]

---

[37] Ellen G. White, *Prophets and Kings* (Mountain View, CA: Pacific Press, 1917), p. 62, emphasis mine.

[38] Ibid., p. 64, emphasis mine.

[39] Ellen G. White, *The Desire of Ages* (Mountain View, CA: Pacific Press, 1898), p. 821, emphasis mine.

[40] Ellen G. White, *The Story of Redemption* (Hagerstown, MD: Review and Herald, 1947), p. 246, emphasis mine.

The time will come when God's people must stand before Him "without a mediator,"[41] a time after probation closes but before Christ returns to claim His own. His children will have been filled with God's Spirit through the latter rain, passed through the furnace of affliction, called the time of Jacob's trouble, and purified of all self-sufficiency. At that time, they perfectly reflect their Savior's likeness and stand as His representatives in the earth, possibly displaying a power akin to that of Christ and Moses.[42] Christ then removes His mediatorial robes and prepares to return for His people. During this time, His faithful followers, purified of all sin, must stand alone.[43] Their righteousness is called **"the righteousness of saints"** (Rev. 19:8). Though they ever credit their Savior for it, it is identified as their own, not Christ's righteousness.

WATER

What about this water that is mixed with the clay? Without water, dust would remain dust and clay would be hard and unyielding in the Potter's hands. No vessels could be formed, no talents conferred. It all starts with the addition of that precious liquid. Inspiration refers to this as the *water of life*. It is also identified as God's mercy, kindness, and compassion—all ours through the merits of Jesus Christ.

"[B]ut whoever drinks of the water that I shall give him shall never thirst, but the water that I shall give him shall be in him a well of water springing up into <u>everlasting life</u>" (John 4:14, MKJV).

"The Spirit and the Bride say, "Come!" Everyone who hears this must also say, "Come!" Come, whoever is thirsty; accept the water of life <u>as a gift,</u> whoever wants it" (Rev. 22:17, GNT).

"Through the merits of Jesus Christ, they realize that nothing is reserved in the heart of God for them but the fountain of the water of life,—<u>tender mercy, loving-kindness, infinite compassion</u>."[44]

This water is powerful! When we fully submit to the master Potter and allow Him to mix as much of this precious water as is needed, He will do amazing things for and through us.

"To everyone who offers himself to the Lord for service, withholding nothing, is given power for the attainment of measureless results. For these

---

[41] Ellen G. White, *The Great Controversy* (Mountain View, CA: Pacific Press, 1911), p. 425.
[42] Revelation 15:3.
[43] Ellen G. White, *The Great Controversy* 1888 (Mountain View, CA: Pacific Press, 1888), p. 425.
[44] Ellen G. White, "Principle Never to be Sacrificed for Peace," *The Bible Echo*, March 26, 1894, emphasis mine.

God will do great things. He will work upon the minds of men so that, even in this world, there shall be seen in their lives a fulfillment of the promise of the future state."[45]

But sometimes God withdraws His gracious Spirit from man, leaving him strangely "alone" to test his resolve, his faith, his determination to honor God or himself.

- ✓ This happened to Hezekiah after he was healed of a terminal illness and visited by powerful rulers to inquire of his God.

"Howbeit in the business of the ambassadors of the princes of Babylon, who sent unto him to enquire of the wonder that was done in the land, God left him, to try him, that he might know all that was in his heart" (2 Chron. 32:31).

- ✓ This happened with Job when Satan accused God of placing a hedge about him (Job 1).
- ✓ This happened with Jesus when dying on the cross (Matt. 27:45–46).

"Faith and hope trembled in the expiring agonies of Christ because God had removed the assurance He had heretofore given His beloved Son of His approbation and acceptance."[46]

This will happen at the close of probation for all people. When God's Spirit is withdrawn from the wicked, their true nature will be seen. When it is withdrawn from the righteous, they will remain righteous and holy still (Rev. 22:11), and able to stand before the Father without a mediator.[47]

> *We should know for ourselves what it means to stand firmly for God, ever learning that which Providence designs to teach us. But too often we think as others think, and do as they do. We are influenced by the habits of our associates. When we depend on finite help to support us, we do not really know our weakness, and when the storm comes, we are overthrown. But when thrust out where we must stand alone, our faith fastens upon the only sure support—the infinite God.*[48]

---

[45] Ellen G. White, *The Ministry of Healing* (Mountain View, CA: Pacific Press, 1905), p. 160, emphasis mine.
[46] Ellen G. White, *Testimonies for the Church, vol. 2* (Mountain View, CA: Pacific Press, 1871), p. 210, emphasis mine.
[47] Ellen G. White, *The Great Controversy* (Mountain View, CA: Pacific Press, 1911), p. 425.
[48] Ellen G. White, "Strength in Humility," *The Youth's Instructor*, January 29, 1903, emphasis mine.

When water is withdrawn from clay, the clay becomes hard and brittle, easily broken. That is the nature of clay. That is what makes clay different from the metals. Clay has never been a substance of strength. Throughout the whole experience of this earthy element, it is Another's merits and Another's handiwork that gives it purpose and life. And if, during use, the clay vessel falls out of the hand of the Master, it breaks (because that is what clay does) and again becomes useless, unless repaired by the compassionate Redeemer. At no point can the clay ever take pride in itself, no matter how great a vessel "unto honor" it may have been made.

The lesson of the clay (dust) is very important in Scripture. And it is no less significant in Daniel 2. Its purpose is more than adding the element of weakness to the iron (Dan. 2:41–42).

POSITIONING OF THE CLAY

As the image is developed in Daniel's explanation to Nebuchadnezzar, metals are used in descending worth to represent weakening world powers. Daniel always respects this order, whether he is going from head to foot or in reverse order. But not so with the clay! He does not treat the clay as a world power, but more as an influence present among the nations. Let's look at some verses in Daniel 2.

The first reference establishes the chronological order. In it, clay is last—in fifth position. In this presentation, the iron and clay are inferred to be "in the last days." However, notice what the prophet does in his two recaps, when he reverses the sequence. He maintains the order of the metals, but places the clay in two different positions, once in fourth and then in third, as if its presence in the image was not confined to the feet alone.

"This image's head was of fine gold; his breast and his arms were of silver; his belly and his thighs were of bronze; his legs were of iron; his feet were part of iron and part of clay" (Dan. 2:32–33, MKJV).

"Then the iron, the clay, the bronze, the silver, and the gold were broken to pieces together. And they became like the chaff of the summer threshing floors" (verse 35, MKJV).

"Because you saw that the stone was cut out of the mountain without hands, and that it crushes the iron, the bronze, the clay, the silver, and the gold, the great God has made known to the king what shall occur after this" (verse 45, MKJV).

There is a fourth position for the clay—implied in the experience of Nebuchadnezzar. Daniel said to the king of Babylon, "**You are this head of** gold" (Dan. 2:38, MKJV). Nebuchadnezzar was a man, just like us, with all the imperfections and weaknesses that come with humanity. But he saw himself as <u>solid</u> gold, as something greater than mere clay, one who didn't need God—as we see in the image he made of himself (Dan. 3) and his statement, "Is not this great Babylon, that I have built?" (Dan. 4:30). With his perspective, who could equal his power and wealth? God had to deal closer with the king a little later to show him his true "metal," to help him understand that his position in the image did not negate his dependence on his Creator. Note Nebuchadnezzar's conclusion after spending time "out in the field." Do you recognize a potter/clay attitude here?

> **And all the people of the earth are counted as nothing; and He does according to His will in the army of heaven, and among the people of the earth. And none can strike His hand, or say to Him, What are You doing? At that time my reason returned to me. And the glory of my kingdom, my honor and brightness returned to me. And my advisers and my lords came for me, and I was established in my kingdom, and excellent majesty was added to me. Now I Nebuchadnezzar praise and exalt and honor the King of heaven, all whose works are truth and His ways judgment. And those who walk in pride He is able to humble. (Dan. 4:35–37, MKJV)**

Apparently, it was not God's purpose to emphasize the human factor in the progression of the kingdoms but rather the descending nature of the empires, the fact that a lesser kingdom would overthrow each world power because God was in control. This was accomplished by using metals. By the time we get to the feet, however, the image has run out of "body armor" and we see the clay element "exposed."

If there is nothing to cover the feet, and the feet are made of clay, then could the whole image have been clay underneath all those metals? Could it be telling us that the whole image was mortal, completely dependent on God to make of it what He would?

We have noted earlier that the four sons of Goliath illustrate the metal kingdoms. Remember who or what the sons were? They were Philistines. "Philistine" in Hebrew means "to roll," possibly referring to their migratory nature. The root word for "rolling," however, adds one more dimension: *to roll (<u>in dust</u>)*. (There's that *dust* word again, only this time associated <u>without</u> water!) These people were not only migratory (Canaan was not their original homeland), they were also a very "earthy" people, worldly, godless. Almost all the time, the Philistines were harassing and plaguing the Israelites. We can expect, then, the kingdoms the Philistine giants represent would not be favorable to God's people, unless Christ was present and in control.

To the proud and self-sufficient, we might think of the uncovered portions of the feet as seeing "the shame of thy nakedness" (Rev. 3:18). (This may be why God asked Moses to remove his sandals while in His presence. Moses was to have nothing "protecting" or "covering" his humanness, his dependency on God (Exod. 3:5).)

The clay in the image starts out mixed with water.

"**And whereas thou sawest the feet and toes, part of <u>potters'</u> clay** [moldable only when wet]**, and part of iron, the kingdom shall be divided; but there shall be in it of the strength of the iron, forasmuch as thou sawest the iron mixed with <u>miry</u> clay**" (Dan. 2:41) (*miry* = wet enough for chariot wheels to get stuck in!).

Eventually, however, the clay in the image dries out.

"**And as the toes of the feet were part of iron, and part of clay, so the kingdom shall be partly strong, and partly brittle**" (Dan. 2:42, MKJV) [Brittleness is a characteristic of dryness].

The mercies and merits of Christ will be withdrawn. And what is left will reveal the true character of the image.

"**Then the iron, the clay, the bronze, the silver, and the gold were broken to pieces together. And they became like the chaff of the summer threshing floors** [very dry]**. And the wind carried them away, so that no place was found for them. And the stone that struck the image became a great mountain and filled the whole earth**" (Dan. 2:35, MKJV).

If you want to see what a person is doing, look at the hands. If you want to see what a person is thinking, look at the eyes. If you want to see where a person is going, look at the feet.

If the whole image of Daniel 2 was clay underneath, Daniel could have put the clay anywhere in his recap and been correct. But why did the clay become apparent only in the feet? What do feet symbolize?

FEET

If you want to see what a person is <u>doing</u>, look at the hands. If you want to see what a person is <u>thinking</u>, look at the eyes. If you want to see where a person is <u>going</u>, look at the feet. They are the first part of our body to enter new territory and the last part to leave. Feet direct the body, consequently they symbolize the <u>directions</u> we take in life, the choices we make.

"But as for me, my feet were almost gone; my steps had well nigh slipped" (Ps. 73:2).

"Thy word is a lamp unto my feet, and a light unto my path" (Ps. 119:105).

"And your feet shod with the preparation of the gospel of peace" (Eph. 6:15).

When Jesus wanted to show His disciples a serious character problem they had, the direction they were heading spiritually, He washed their feet. When Mary wanted to show her love for her Lord and prepare His body for burial, she anointed His feet, as well as His head. These choices we make affect our <u>character</u>. So, seeing the clay in the feet could help us understand something about the true nature of the image, why all the kingdoms fell and why the whole image will eventually be replaced by a different system. This becomes clearer as we apply the Bible's figurative use of clay.

When Jesus washed the dust from the disciples' feet, He was, in effect, removing that which represented their weakness. They were trusting in themselves rather than in their Savior who was in their midst.

> *"He that is washed needeth not save to wash his feet, but is clean every whit." These words mean more than bodily cleanliness. Christ is still speaking of the higher cleansing as illustrated by the lower. He who came from the bath was clean, but the sandaled feet soon became dusty, and again needed to be washed. So Peter and his brethren had been washed in the great fountain opened for sin and uncleanness. Christ acknowledged them as His. But temptation had led them into evil, and they still needed His cleansing grace. When Jesus girded Himself with a towel to wash the dust from their feet, He desired by that very act to wash the alienation, jealousy, and pride from their hearts. This was of far more consequence than the washing of their dusty feet. With the spirit they then had, not one of them was prepared for communion with Christ. Until brought into a state of humility and love, they were not prepared to partake of the paschal supper, or to share in the memorial service which Christ was about to institute. Their hearts must be cleansed. Pride and self-seeking create dissension and hatred, but all this Jesus washed away in washing their feet. A change of feeling was brought about. Looking upon them, Jesus could say, "Ye are clean."*

Now there was union of heart, love for one another. They had become humble and teachable. Except Judas, each was ready to concede to another the highest place. Now with subdued and grateful hearts they could receive Christ's words.[49]

Since various metals covered every other part of the image, hiding the clay-like features, the weakness and dependency of man are not defining issues in the description of the four previous kingdoms, but when discussing the demise of the whole image, the clay-like features become prominent. So, we look at the feet of the great image to see where it is going, to see if we want to go with it, or go somewhere else.

DANIEL AND REVELATION

We know that both books of Daniel and Revelation are to be studied together. Each sheds light on the other. What about this time of the feet spoken about in Daniel 2? It ends with Rome closely associating with clay in the last days, just before Christ sets up His kingdom. John picks up the Rome element but doesn't mention clay *per se*. He does talk about an "earthly" element, however, working in conjunction with the (iron) beast (Rev. 13:11–18). Could this be the "clay"?

John's metaphor is more Egypt-like.

- The 2-horned beast speaks like a dragon (Rev. 13:11), which more specifically is *cunning and deceptive* (Rev. 12:9; see also Gen. 3:1 *[subtle, cunning]*; Exod. 1:8–10 *[wisely, shrewdly]*).
- The only way the faithful will be delivered in that day is by a mighty Leader bringing ***plagues*** upon this Egypt-like power (Rev. 15) until they are able to "go worship the Lord freely."
- The delivered sing the ***song of Moses and the Lamb*** (Rev. 15:3).

Where do God's people go after being delivered? To that heavenly place where "there shall be no more the Canaanite in the house of the Lord of hosts" (Zech. 14:21).

Is Revelation 12 and 13 talking about a real Egypt? No. Egypt had her day, as did Babylon and others. But that which characterized Egypt could be seen in other nations or world powers. Is it possible a power in the final days of the iron kingdom's rule could characterize Egypt though not being

---

[49] Ellen G. White, *The Desire of Ages* (Mountain View, CA: Pacific Press, 1898), p. 646, emphasis mine.

Egypt or Egyptian? Seems fair—especially when we read Revelation 11:8 and Mrs. White's comment on it.

"And their dead bodies shall lie in the street of the great city, which spiritually is called Sodom and Egypt, where also our Lord was crucified" (Rev 11:8).

> *According to the words of the prophet, then, a little before the year 1798 some power of Satanic origin and character would rise to make war upon the Bible. And in the land where the testimony of God's two witnesses should thus be silenced, there would be manifest the atheism of the Pharaoh [Egypt], and the licentiousness of Sodom. This prophecy has received a most exact and striking fulfillment in the history of France.*[50]

Anyone or anything that duplicates the characteristics of the original can be called by the name of the original. Thus, John the Baptist was called Elijah, as will God's faithful in the end of time. And so with France. She met the basic characteristics of Egypt and was called Egypt.

However, the reason for an interest in an Egypt-like power in the last days goes much deeper. The Egypt-like characteristics multiply.

EGYPT AS A REFUGE

In spite of the fact that Egypt was a heathen nation, she was used many times as a <u>refuge</u>, a place of safety.

- Abram (Gen. 12:10)
- Jacob's family (Gen. 42:1–2)
- Hadad (1 Kings 11:17)
- Jeroboam (1 Kings 11:40)
- Urijah (Jer. 26:21)
- Joseph and Mary with Jesus (Matt. 2:13)

And many of those times, God Himself opened the way! Mrs. White explained His purpose for sending Israel to Egypt:

> *The assurance, "Fear not to go down into Egypt; for I will there make of thee a great nation," was significant. The promise had been given to Abraham of a posterity numberless as the stars, but as yet the chosen*

---

[50] Ellen G. White, *The Great Controversy* 1888 (Mountain View, CA: Pacific Press, 1888), p. 269, emphasis mine.

> *people had increased but slowly. And the land of Canaan now offered no field for the development of such a nation as had been foretold. It was in the possession of powerful heathen tribes that were not to be dispossessed until 'the fourth generation.' If the descendants of Israel were here to become a numerous people, they must either drive out the inhabitants of the land or disperse themselves among them. The former, according to the divine arrangement, they could not do; and should they mingle with the Canaanites, they would be in danger of being seduced into idolatry. Egypt, however, offered the conditions necessary to the fulfillment of the divine purpose. A section of country well-watered and fertile was open to them there, affording every advantage for their speedy increase. And the antipathy they must encounter in Egypt on account of their occupation—for every shepherd was "an abomination unto the Egyptians"—would enable them to remain a distinct and separate people and would thus serve to shut them out from participation in the idolatry of Egypt.*[51]

And, of all the places Joseph could have been directed to keep Mary and her baby safe, Egypt was again chosen by God.

"*In like manner Joseph received warning to flee into Egypt with Mary and the child. And the angel said, 'Be thou there until I bring thee word: for Herod will seek the young child to destroy Him.' Joseph obeyed without delay, setting out on the journey by night for greater security.*"[52]

No other kingdom had this strong scriptural association of being a <u>refuge, a haven of safety</u>.

EGYPT AND RELIGIOUS TOLERATION

A second characteristic of Egypt is her religious toleration.

Egypt was a religious kingdom, albeit pagan. She depended heavily upon her mystic advisors as how to operate the kingdom. The power these magicians and astrologers held with the pharaohs was evident during the drama of the great exodus. But, initially, she was tolerant to Joseph's religion, for had not his God shown favor to the nation through the interpretation of Pharaoh's dream? And had not Joseph's God given him exceptional skill in affairs of state?

---

[51] Ellen G. White, *Patriarchs and Prophets* (Mountain View, CA: Pacific Press, 1890), p. 232, emphasis mine.
[52] Ellen G. White, *The Desire of Ages* (Mountain View, CA: Pacific Press, 1898), p. 64, emphasis mine.

It was the Israelite's occupation the Egyptians couldn't stand, for Joseph's family were herdsmen and shepherds. This actually proved a blessing. It helped keep the two nations separate.

> **And Joseph said to his brothers and to his father's house, I will go up and show Pharaoh, and say to him, My brothers and my father's house, who were in the land of Canaan, have come to me. And the men are shepherds, for they have been men of cattle. And they have brought their flocks and their herds and all that they have. And it shall be when Pharaoh shall call you, and shall say, What is your occupation? Then you shall say, Your servants have been men of cattle from our youth even until now, both we and our fathers, so that you may live in the land of Goshen, for every shepherd is an abomination to the Egyptians. (Gen. 46:31–34, MKJV)**

A <u>highly religious government</u> combined with <u>religious toleration</u> is another thing that sets Egypt apart from the "metal" kingdoms of Daniel 2. The other nations may have tolerated, or even invited, the presence of God's people in their borders (as Babylon did), but these were worldly kingdoms whose leaders often thought of themselves as gods. When Rome converted to Catholicism and became a religious nation, toleration for God's people was not a characteristic.

EGYPT AND DIPLOMACY

> **And the sons of Israel were fruitful, and increased very much, and multiplied, and became exceedingly mighty. And the land was filled with them. And there arose a new king over Egypt, who did not know Joseph. And he said to his people, Behold, the people of the sons of Israel are many and mightier than we. Come, <u>let us deal wisely with them</u>, lest they multiply, and it will be when there comes a war, they join also to our enemies, and fight against us, and get out of the land. (Exod. 1:7–10, MKJV)**

Diplomacy has been a common characteristic of leaders. What makes Egypt different in this respect is her purpose in using it. Today, when conflict threatens the security of a nation, its leaders will parley back and forth with compromises to agree on mutually beneficial arrangements. We call this "cold war" tactics. If this doesn't work, then the contest switches to military strength. The Egyptian leaders perceived the nation of Israel as "mightier" than themselves and felt the security of Egypt was at risk. Until a true assessment of Israel's military strength was made, diplomacy would be used to keep the foreign nation comfortable.

But national security was not the only factor. God had blessed the Israelites in their temporary home. And in blessing them, He blessed also the nation who harbored them. Egypt's leaders recognized great gain in controlling this powerful and prolific people. They didn't want them to "**get out of the land**" (Exod. 1:10, MKJV).

"**Let us deal wisely with them**" (ibid, KJV), they said. The leaders thought it prudent to approach the Israelites carefully, in a way that would not upset them. (They thought of the Israelites as a powerful people.) They must first make sure the Israelites' ability to retaliate is diffused. Egypt's intent was not just to provide <u>national security</u> but also to <u>control</u> for national benefit. And she would do it, initially, through <u>statesmanship</u>.

Through diplomacy, Egypt was able not only to keep a mightier nation from revolting but also to position them for complete subjection.

EGYPT'S TURNCOAT NATURE

The picture is striking. We see at one point a small group of people, seventy in number, accepted with smiles and open arms. They were highly respected (though their occupation was not appreciated) and given the most fertile land the country had to offer. Then we see that same group of people, now numbering in the millions, treated and controlled as slaves, with absolutely no respect. And all smiles are gone. What happened?

The true nature of Egypt has come to full fruition. Her true character is seen ... when the Spirit of God is removed.

We are not given the details on exactly how she subjected a nation greater in number and power than herself. But what is made clear is the fact that Egypt will dominate, she will control, no matter who or what. That is where she always goes.

In Revelation 12, we see Rome described as a "**great red dragon, having seven heads and ten horns, and seven crowns upon his heads**" (verse 3). Here the iron kingdom has taken on the ecclesiastical nature Daniel foresaw (Dan. 7:23-25). And in the same chapter, we begin to see evidence of the Egyptian influence. The earth helps the woman (God's church). It becomes a "haven" country, a place where God's people could flee to when food was scarce or oppression was heavy. Do you see a parallel here?

> **And the woman** [God's church] **fled** [sought for a refuge] **into the wilderness, where she had a place prepared by God, so that they might nourish** [fatten up with food] **her there a thousand, two**

hundred and sixty days …. And two wings of a great eagle were given to the woman, so that she might fly into the wilderness, into her place, where she is nourished for a time and times and half a time, from the serpent's [oppressing] **face.** (Rev. 12:6, 14, MKJV)

This REFUGE included many different places. One of them, we understand, was the new world of the Americas, discovered during this time—a very fertile country (as was Goshen, the place in Egypt given for the Israelites to occupy). John continues to describe this new land with the capacity to "swallow" water. Clay is the only element in Daniel 2 that can absorb water—up to four times the volume of clay.

"And the earth helped the woman, and the earth opened her mouth, and swallowed up the flood which the dragon cast out of his mouth" (Rev. 12:16).

John adds even more details about the time when the feet are *part of iron and part of clay*. Revelation 13:1–8 describes the iron portion, a religious power rising "out of the sea," blaspheming God, accepting the worship of man, making war with the saints, and getting its power from the dragon (Satan himself). Verses 11–17 describe the clay portion, a contrasting power rising "out of the earth." It, too, has spiritual overtones, yet its power over the people seems to be more with mystic fascination and deception, for it speaks "as a dragon" [Greek for *dragon: a fabulous kind of serpent (perhaps as supposed to fascinate)*], "doeth great wonders," and *deceives them that dwell on the earth.*

Remember, the intent of the Egyptian leaders was to *"deal wisely"* with the people for the purpose of controlling them (Exod. 1:10). We should see this friendly, refuge-type clay influence gaining some sort of civil power over the masses.

"And he causeth all, both small and great, rich and poor, free and bond, to receive a mark in their right hand, or in their foreheads: And that no man might buy or sell, save he that had the mark, or the name of the beast, or the number of his name" (Rev. 13:16–17).

This power will be used against God's people.

"And he had power to give life unto the image of the beast, that the image of the beast should both speak, and cause that as many as would not worship the image of the beast should be killed" (Rev 13:15).

EGYPT + CLAY = MAN

We have been studying the same event in both apocalyptic books, using different metaphors. It is the similarity of both that makes this possible.

Egypt reveals the true nature of clay. And clay reveals the true nature of Egypt.

Man was first made in God's image, and man was made from clay. As man was to reveal the qualities of his Maker, so we should find clay doing the same. By combining all that we have studied in Daniel and Revelation, we get this image of man, when the Spirit of God is in him:

> Like clay to water, man has a natural affinity to the Spirit of God
>
> He becomes a refuge to those hurting and in need
>
> He nurtures others
>
> Though himself spiritual, he is tolerant of the beliefs of others
>
> He speaks wisely and carefully

But we also see that as man begins to separate himself from God's spirit, a change occurs.

> He uses his powers to deceive.
>
> He desires to control others
>
> He will eventually kill if he cannot control

When that happens, he falls and is broken, with no one to put him back together. He has rejected the only Spirit that could help him.

THE UNITED STATES

We have long taught that the United States was John's beast that comes up out of the earth and provides a haven for the woman. We refer to the "land" or "wilderness" (a fertile land almost completely devoid of people where the persecuted could be nurtured safely), and the beast with lamblike horns (possibly identifying it as a "Christian" nation in its infancy—the horns were "lamblike," not "ram-like," signifying they were from a younger animal). John gives a lot of clues. Now we see that Daniel 2 adds to that interpretation significantly.

As we consider the USA filling the Egypt-like role, we are led to consider also the purpose God had for leading His people to that heathen land. Heathen? It's easy for us to see Egypt as a heathen nation, but what about the "lamblike" beast of Revelation? Didn't that mean it was Christian? No. It really wasn't a "lamblike" *beast*. It just had lamblike *horns,* meaning it used Christian principles to rule by (in Scripture horns = power). It was really a **beast** that came up out of the earth. The Greek word used for "beast" here means a dangerous animal (venomous, wild).

This is not describing a house pet or domestic creature! The United States was not intended to be the Promised Land for God's people, a place of retirement, but the place God intended for them to be <u>nurtured and to grow in numbers</u> **prior** to their "taking on" their inheritance. Let's look again at God's purpose for sending Israel into Egypt.

> *The assurance, "Fear not to go down into Egypt; for I will there make of thee a great nation," was significant. The promise had been given to Abraham of a posterity numberless as the stars, but as yet the chosen people had increased but slowly. And the land of Canaan now offered no field for the development of such a nation as had been foretold .... Egypt, however, offered the conditions necessary to the fulfillment of the divine purpose. A section of country well-watered and fertile was open to them there, affording every advantage for their speedy increase.[53]*

Apparently, numbers and size are sometimes important in God's program. Could His intent for planting the remnant church on American soil be to feed and nurture her and help her grow in numbers for giving the last-day message to a dying world? Has the church used the freedoms and resources provided by the United States to launch and support a worldwide message? Where did our medical and educational programs start? Where did our worldwide radio and television ministries begin? Where is most of the world church's monetary wealth? This country has definitely been a haven and growing field for God's people.

But when the day comes that the church is big and strong enough, a power to be reckoned with in the world, she will lose her favor with "the pharaohs" and efforts will be made to "control" her. That is the nature of Egypt. It is then that the beast with "lamblike" horns will speak "as a dragon" and try to control a kingdom mightier than herself.

The "land of the free" will turn against God's church but not initially with force of arms (typical to the kingdom of iron), but rather with the voice of a "dragon" (a fabulous kind of *serpent* [perhaps as supposed to *fascinate*]). We are shown the serpent in action in heaven, where a third of the angels were deceived (Rev. 12:4), and in the Garden of Eden (Gen. 3), where our first parents fell. The serpent uses truth riddled with lies and deceptions and is very effective. In Revelation 13, he again is using miracles and mystic powers (through the beast with lamblike horns) to convince the world of his "authority." The pharaoh that "knew not Joseph" said, **"Come, let us deal craftily with them"** (Exod. 1:10, LITV). That type

---
[53] Ellen G. White, *Patriarchs and Prophets* (Mountain View, CA: Pacific Press, 1890), p. 232, emphasis mine.

of "wisdom" was for the purpose of total control. That's the nature of the wild and venomous beast, the beast that is not controlled by God's Spirit!

Consider this characteristic of Egypt of old. Is this the destiny of the United States when she repudiates God's law?

> *Of all nations presented in Bible history, Egypt most boldly denied the existence of the living God and resisted His commands. No monarch ever ventured upon more open and high-handed rebellion against the authority of Heaven than did the king of Egypt. When the message was brought him by Moses, in the name of the Lord, Pharaoh proudly answered: "Who is Jehovah, that I should obey his voice to let Israel go? I know not Jehovah, neither will I let Israel go." [Exodus 5:2.] This is atheism; and the nation represented by Egypt would give voice to a similar denial of the claims of the living God and would manifest a like spirit of unbelief and defiance.*[54]

Daniel says the clay and iron will work together. Revelation says the beast with lamblike horns will work together with the beast that had a wound and was healed. And the first beast will deny the claims of God, make an image after its own likeness, give it life, and have it control the world. We have noticed that Daniel and John use different metaphors to describe the ecclesiastical and political powers—churchcraft (the first beast of Revelation 13: Rome) and statecraft (the second beast in that chapter: the USA, represented by mystic Egypt)—affecting God's people in the last days.

> *"The mingling of churchcraft and statecraft is represented by the iron and the clay. This union is weakening all the power of the churches. This investing the church with the power of the state will bring evil results."*[55]

But these metaphors appear to be strongly related. Is there any place the Bible ties these two metaphors—clay and Egypt—together in discussing world prowess? Yes! In the last giant. The Egyptian giant.

THE FINAL GIANT

Remember the difficulty we encountered in Daniel 2, to determine the placement of the clay? At one point it seems to come at the end and, a little later, Daniel places it in the midst of the metals (Dan. 2:35, 45). We have a similar difficulty in placing this last giant. Like with the first four

---

[54] Ellen G. White, *The Great Controversy 1888* (Mountain View, CA: Pacific Press, 1888), p. 269, emphasis mine.
[55] Ellen G. White, *SDA Bible Commentary, vol. 4* (Washington, DC: Review and Herald, 1955), pp. 1168–1169, emphasis mine.

behemoths, the Bible gives two accounts where we can read about the Egyptian giant. One is in 2 Samuel 23:21 and the other is in 1 Chronicles 11:23. The first reference is in Samuel's account, where the Egyptian is placed <u>after</u> the encounter with Goliath's four sons. But the last reference in the Chronicles places him <u>before</u> the fray with the Philistines! Hmmm ….

And, as the clay was different than the metals, the giant is different than the sons of Goliath. They were Philistines. He was Egyptian! Does the Bible give a tie-in with Egypt and clay? You can be sure of it! God's people were in Egypt for 400 years. They received the harboring, the nurturing, the religious tolerance. Then they saw what happened when its leader knew not God. The Spirit of God was rejected and the spirit of dominion entered. For at least the latter part of those 400 years, they were forced into manual labor.

> **And there arose a new king over Egypt, who did not know Joseph. And he said to his people, Behold, the people of the sons of Israel are many and mightier than we. Come, let us deal slyly with them, lest they multiply, and it will be when there comes a war, they join also to our enemies, and fight against us, and get out of the land. And they set taskmasters over them to afflict them with their burdens. And they built treasure cities for Pharaoh, Pithon and Raamses. (Exod. 1:8–11, MKJV)**

In Exodus 5, we can zone in on exactly what they were doing to build these cities. They were making bricks—out of clay! At least to God's people, there is a definite association of Egypt with clay. And it is not positive.

> **And the king of Egypt said to them, Moses and Aaron, Why do you keep the people from their work? Get to your burdens! And Pharaoh said, Behold, the people of the land now are many, and you make them rest from their burdens. And Pharaoh commanded the taskmasters of the people and their officers the same day, saying, You shall no more give the people straw to make brick, as before. Let them go and gather straw for themselves. (Exod. 5:4–7, MKJV)**

> *The most common building material of that country was sun-dried brick; the walls of the finest edifices were made of this, and then faced with stone; and the manufacture of brick employed great numbers of the bondmen. Cut straw being intermixed with the clay, to hold it*

together, large quantities of straw were required for the work; the king now directed that no more straw be furnished; the laborers must find it for themselves, while the same amount of brick should be exacted.[56]

Let's look more closely at this Egyptian and see what we can learn about the last-day power Daniel calls clay and John refers to as Egypt.

> **And he slew an Egyptian,**
> **a man of *great* stature [a goodly man],**
> **five cubits high;**
> **and in the Egyptian's hand *was* a spear like a weaver's beam;**
> **and he went down to him with a staff,**
> **and plucked the spear out of the Egyptian's hand,**
> **and slew him with his own spear.**
> 1 Chronicles 11:23

And he slew an Egyptian...

This Egyptian we find threatening God's people is out of place. He was not a Canaanite, needing to defend his turf. Nor was he part of an invading army trying to extend their conquests. He apparently wasn't even among a band of marauders seeking to advantage themselves by the wealth of the land. He appeared to be alone. Yet still he portrayed a danger to God's people. The mighty men of David's army were not known to kill anyone who wasn't an Israelite. There had to be a threat to the nation or to their leader to arouse them for combat. There must have been some reason the Egyptian was out of his element and intimidating God's people. What could it have been?

... A man of great stature [a goodly man] ...

This enemy was described in very positive words: "great stature" (as referring to prominence, someone to respect), or "a goodly man," as described in a parallel passage, 2 Samuel 23:21 (meaning "handsome, comely, favored"). Why describe an enemy in such a positive way? What was it that made this giant so attractive? Was it the fact that he was an Egyptian? Not likely. It appears that the Israelites would have a difficult time thinking positively about one who reminded them of their Egyptian experience. Long years of slavery would not be easy to forget. We get the

---

[56] Ellen G. White, *Patriarchs and Prophets* (Mountain View, CA: Pacific Press, 1890), p. 258, emphasis mine.

idea that this giant had something more going for him than just the fact that he was an Egyptian.

Moses was an Egyptian. He was born in Egypt and educated there and adopted by the royal family, destined to lead the nation. But Moses was also an Israelite. Could this giant have similar characteristics? Perhaps he, too, would have a dual "citizenship," fully "Egyptian" and fully "Christian." This could explain how he was found "within the camp" and as a threat to the nation.

Other than being somewhat attractive, there are only two other characteristics that describe this Egyptian: his height and his spear. Yet (as in geometry) two points are enough to establish a direction (see also Deut. 19:15). Let's see where they take us. Maybe we can see why he was described so positively.

Five cubits high

These three words immediately following the thought referring to "prominence," "someone to respect," and replaced by "a goodly man" in the parallel passage (2 Sam. 23:21), give us a major clue as to the nature of this enemy. (When the Bible gives a clue, we are expected to search it out!)

Was there anything else in Scripture to compare "five cubits high" with, something that might help us understand who or what this giant really represented? The first and most prominent reference was to the wall around the courtyard, also **five cubits high** and made of fine, twined linen (Exod. 27:18). As we are faced with this wall before entering the sanctuary, we are impressed with three things: color, substance, and height.

1. Color: WHITE. Often referring to **purity, cleanliness** (Isa. 1:18).
2. Substance: FINE, TWINED LINEN. The **righteousness of the saints** (Rev. 19:8).
3. Height: FIVE CUBITS. Vertical ascent deals with prominence, respect, man's relation to God. A cubit was the measurement of part of a person's body, from the tip of the elbow to the end of the fingers (about eighteen inches). When this distance is multiplied by five, it defines the height to which a person could reach on tiptoe (usually within an inch or so—try it! Every person's "cubit" may be different, but the result is the same!). In effect, five cubits is **the extent (or potential) to which a person can reach in any direction.**

Putting this together, we get the picture that the courtyard wall of five cubits (about seven-and-a-half feet in our language) was a figure of the righteous character God would develop in His saint if she/he entered the school, the potential mankind can reach with God's help. In another passage, we are told who was to be clothed in this "righteousness."

"**Let Your priests be clothed with righteousness, and Your saints shout for joy**" (Ps. 132:9, MKJV).

A priest was a servant of God, devoted to lifelong ministry to the body of Christ, in the capacity of minister, teacher (Deut. 24:8), doctor, or musician (1 Chron. 9:33). Could it be that this Egyptian was associated, or appeared to be associated, with some kind of ministry, perhaps as an instructor in righteousness?

If so, this would not be the only time imposters have tried to upset the family of God in this way. Look at Zimri, a noble in Israel (Num. 25:14), or Judas, highly regarded by the disciples,[57] or Jezebel, a spiritual leader in Thyatira (Rev. 2:6, 20). All these were considered people of rank, prestige, and talent, and were given responsible positions in the kingdom, group, or church. And yet they were all enemies of truth. (See also Matt. 7:15; Acts 20:29–30).

Is the Egyptian masquerading as a priest or teacher? We can only assume at this point but at least it is a possibility. Priests are definitely someone we are to look up to—not by nature of their person but by nature of their position.

Five cubits is not really very tall for giants. Og, the king of Bashan, the first giant named in the Bible, slept in a bed that was four cubits wide and nine cubits long! Even if Og was only eight cubits tall, that would make him a whopping twelve feet! Goliath was six cubits and a span (the spread of the fingers). It's not likely the Egyptian's physical height alone gave him his prominence. Let's go to the second point.

And in the Egyptian's hand was a spear like a weaver's beam

It was what the giant held in his hand that clarified his purpose. The hand has always been used as a figure of our works. We may have all kinds of things going on in our minds, but what we actually **do** is often that by which we are judged.

"**A man had two sons; and he came to the first and said, Son, go work in my vineyard today. He answered and said, I will not. But afterwards he**

---
[57] Ellen G. White, *The Desire of Ages* (Mountain View, CA: Pacific Press, 1898), p. 717.

repented and went. And he came to the second and said likewise. And he answered and said, I go, sir; and did not go. Which of the two did the will of his father?" (Matt. 21:28–31, MKJV).

"Whatever your hand finds to do, do it with all your might; for there is no work, nor plan, nor knowledge, nor wisdom, in the grave where you go" (Eccles. 9:10, MKJV).

"And he causeth all, both small and great, rich and poor, free and bond, to receive a mark in their right hand, or in their foreheads" (Rev. 13:16).

When God chose Moses to deliver His people from Egyptian bondage, Moses believed he didn't have the resources to finish what God would have him begin. God asked him, "What is that in your hand?" (Exod. 4:2, MKJV). God used the very tools Moses was familiar with to approach Pharaoh.

What did the giant hold in his hand? A spear like a weaver's beam. This is the third giant described as having such a weapon. Lahmi and Goliath were the other two. (Note: Again, with this giant, no spearhead is mentioned, suggesting the "killing" part is either unperceived or considered insignificant.) In each case, the spear's shaft was associated with that which is used to make cloth, from <u>the beginning to the end</u>. Again, we are presented with the concept of <u>garments</u>! As we have noted earlier in this study, *garments* are a reference to <u>*character building*</u> or <u>*education in righteousness*</u>. Who is it that helps us develop character? Our parents, teachers, friends, spiritual leaders, the angel host. Are these ones we should be able to trust and look up to? Remember, though, this "weaver's beam" was perceived as a weapon!

The Egyptian, then, appears to be representing someone of commanding appearance who establishes himself as a teacher of righteousness, although an enemy of Christ's people. Why would we think of an enemy as our friend, wanting to help us, someone we would let our children be around? Remember the positive characteristics of Egypt?

1. A place of safety and nurturing
2. Religious tolerance
3. Diplomatic

The Egyptian is described as "goodly," "handsome," "attractive." Up to this point, he is seen simply as a clay vessel. He must have been perceived at first as a helper, someone friendly and spiritual, someone in whose company we can feel safe and nurtured—possibly a teacher or counselor or minister. We can picture this huge, good-looking man coming to us smiling. His size and "weapon" were associated with life and righteousness, the coverings of priests and the redeemed. All seems so good.

Then something happens. The life-giving element of water disappears from the clay, leaving it hard and brittle. The smile has changed, and we find ourselves being manipulated, confined, enslaved. We remember Jonestown, South Africa, and Waco, Texas. We are trapped and who can deliver us?

"As I beheld him [Satan]*, his chin was resting upon his left hand. He appeared to be in deep thought. A smile was upon his countenance, which made me tremble, it was so full of evil and satanic slyness. This smile is the one he wears just before he makes sure of his victim, and as he fastens the victim in his snare, this smile grows horrible."*[58]

In Israel's day, only Benaiah, the son of Jehoiada, saw through this façade and was able to confront the giant. Who is this deliverer?

THE DELIVERER

The Egyptian giant was killed by one of David's men, a man zealous for the kingdom of God. Perhaps he alone saw the Egyptian as a threat to the nation. Others either didn't see, didn't care, or felt impotent to make a difference. By what we pondered thus far, it appears that the giant presented himself, figuratively, as a teacher of righteousness (five cubits high), someone having mystical powers (Egyptian) to direct and inspire the church (staff like a weaver's beam). He came alone and seemed harmless (there was no spearhead described or noted). He appeared attractive. He was not perceived immediately as an enemy but possibly as a teacher of God's people. Such imposters have ever been a threat to God's people down through the ages.

Ahab brought Jezebel, a heathen woman, into the kingdom of God. Her wicked influence was ever a galling yoke to the nation. But, though her dedication to evil was never abated, many of those around her believed she was an asset to the kingdom.

A very interesting Old Testament text sheds light on the possibility that Ahab's wife may have assumed a teaching position in the kingdom of Israel, as a counterfeit instructor in righteousness, a false teacher. As we have studied earlier, true education addresses the whole potential of man, on this earth and for the earth to come. It affects the head <u>to reflect the</u>

---

[58] Ellen G. White, *Early Writings* (Washington, DC: Review and Herald, 1882), p. 153, emphasis mine.

mind and thoughts of God, the hands to do works of righteousness and the feet to walk in the paths of obedience and faith. Christ was the True Teacher. His death on the cross was a complete sacrifice, atoning for every aspect of mankind, His own **head** pierced by a crown of thorns and His **hands** and **feet** impaled to the cross by Roman spikes. The evening before, when He was washing the feet of His disciples, Peter, catching a glimpse of the significance of the act asked his Master to wash not only his **feet**, but his **hands** and **head** as well (John 13:8–9). He wanted every part of his life to be clean. And after Christ's resurrection, to assure His friends of His reality, Jesus showed them His **hands** and **feet** (**His head** was obvious) (Luke 24:39–40).

As we learned earlier, somebody saw through Jezebel's disguise and threw her out of her palace window. Remember what the dogs left of her body to bury—the skull, feet, and palms of her hands.

Was this supposed to tell us something about the woman? Jezebel, though not an Egyptian, represented the same devotion to the powers of evil as did that Egyptian giant. Yet she is presented in Revelation as a teacher of righteousness, a prophetess even! The New Testament church in Thyatira didn't seem to feel threatened by her presence either, though she was leading them astray.

"But I have a few things against you because you allow that woman Jezebel to teach, she saying herself to be a prophetess, and to cause My servants to go astray, and to commit fornication, and to eat idol-sacrifices" (Rev. 2:20, MKJV).

The Egyptian giant and the clay represent a peculiar threat to God's people in the end of time. Note Christ's warning for those living in the last days.

"For false Christs and false prophets will arise and show great signs and wonders; so much so that, if it were possible, they would deceive even the elect" (Matt. 24:24, MKJV).

True education, however, empowers us against false education, it helps us to know God and do His bidding.

> *In His prayer to the Father, Christ gave to the world a lesson which should be graven on mind and soul. "This is life eternal," He said, "that they might know Thee the only true God, and Jesus Christ, whom Thou hast sent." John 17:3. This is true education. It imparts power. The experimental knowledge of God and of Jesus Christ whom He has sent, transforms man into the image of God. It gives to man the mastery of himself, bringing every impulse and passion of the lower*

> *nature under the control of the higher powers of the mind. It makes its possessor a son of God and an heir of heaven. It brings him into communion with the mind of the Infinite, and opens to him the rich treasures of the universe.*[59]

No wonder, then, before the end can come (Matt. 24:14), education **must be restored to its rightful position in the church!**

> *Before we can carry the message of present truth in all its fullness to other countries we must first break every yoke. We must come into the line of <u>true education</u>, walking in the wisdom of God, and not in the wisdom of the world. God calls for messengers who will be true reformers. We must educate, educate, to prepare a people who will understand the message, and then give the message to the world.*[60]

Just why this is so, is explained:

"True education is the preparation of the physical, mental, and moral powers for the performance of every duty; it is the training of body, mind, and soul for divine service. This is the education that will endure unto eternal life."[61]

Because the Egyptian giant represents a <u>false</u>, deceptive education, the one who delivers us from the giant must have something to do with <u>true</u> education. Let's see how the Bible describes Israel's champion, Benaiah, the son of Jehoiada.

BENAIAH THE SON OF JEHOIADA

> Benaiah the son of Jehoiada, the son of a mighty man of Kabzeel, had done many acts. He killed two lion-like men of Moab. He also went down and killed a lion in a pit on a snowy day. And he killed an Egyptian, a man of stature, five cubits high. And in the Egyptian's hand was a spear like a weaver's beam. And he went down to him with a staff and wrenched the spear out of the Egyptians hand, and killed him with his own spear. (1 Chron. 11:22–23, MKJV)

In this man, we see one custom-designed by God to confront the Egyptian. This man was no second-class soldier.

---

[59] Ellen G. White, *Christ's Object Lessons* (Washington, DC: Review and Herald, 1900), p. 114, emphasis mine.

[60] Ellen G. White, "A Missionary Education," *The Review and Herald*, February 6, 1908, emphasis mine.

[61] Ellen G. White, *Christ's Object Lessons* (Washington, DC: Review and Herald, 1900), p. 330, emphasis mine.

"And Benaiah the son of Jehoiada was over both the Cherethites [life guardsmen] **and the Pelethites** [couriers or official messengers]**; and David's sons were chief rulers**" (2 Sam. 8:18).

We learn of Benaiah's training and equipping as we study the information given about him. It describes those God prepares for the last-day battle against the beast with lamblike horns.

Benaiah comes from two Hebrew words and means "*Jah has built [or made].*" One of the words is using a special name of God and the other word is an action word, something God has done. The first name employed is a twist on Jehovah, the national name of God. There are only forty-five verses in the whole Old Testament that use this special form of the name (Strong's H3050), whereas there are 5,521 verses that use the more prominent name of Jehovah (Strong's H3068). That is less than one verse out of 122. It was first coined in a song expressing Israel's joy in being delivered from the Egyptians. Note the response Israel had in the song:

"**The LORD**[3050] **is my strength and song, and he is become my salvation: he is my God, and I will prepare him an habitation; my father's God, and I will exalt him**" (Exod. 15:2).

> *Contemplating the Lord's graciousness, we want to enjoy His presence and exalt Him before the world. Preparing Him "an habitation" includes a body temple (John 2:21, 1 Cor. 6:19), the closest and most intimate habitation possible. And the place we prepare will be our very best (most healthful, strong, and alert). This is the scope of medical missionary work!*

Contemplating the Lord's graciousness, we want to enjoy His presence and exalt Him before the world. Preparing Him "an habitation" includes a body temple (John 2:21, 1 Cor. 6:19), the closest and most intimate habitation possible. And the place we prepare will be our very best (most healthful, strong, and alert). This is the scope of **medical missionary work!**

The second part of Benaiah's name is an action word, meaning "*to build, make, repair, obtain children*" (Strong's H1129). It, too, is a special variation but this time on the word "*make.*" During Creation Week, God (Elohim) *"made"* (Strong's H6213) many things. But the very first thing God (Jehovah) *"made"* (Strong's H1129) was a woman, a helpmeet and companion for Adam (Gen. 2:22)—His <u>last</u> act in the six days of Creation Week.

"And the rib, which the LORD God had taken from man, made[1129] he a woman, and brought her unto the man" (Gen. 2:22).

In Proverbs 24:27, we are told <u>when</u> it is appropriate to "build [or make[1129]]."

"Prepare thy work without, and make it fit for thyself in the field; and afterwards build[1129] [make] thine house" (Prov. 24:27).

IT IS THE <u>LAST</u> WORK

In Genesis 2, after everything else had been set in place, God "made" a woman, with the potential of developing the seed of her husband into a new being. In Proverbs 24, after everything else has been set in place, we are to "build" our house, obtain children, increase our family. This use of the word "build" takes us also to Isaiah 58:12, the divine purpose for medical missionary work.

"And they that shall be of thee shall build[1129] the old waste places: thou shalt raise up the foundations of many generations; and thou shalt be called, The repairer of the breach, The restorer of paths to dwell in" (Isa. 58:12).

> [After quoting Isaiah 58:12–14] *Thus genuine medical missionary work is bound up inseparably with the keeping of God's commandments, of which the Sabbath is especially mentioned, since it is the great memorial of God's creative work. Its observance is bound up with the work of restoring the moral image of God in man. This is the ministry which God's people are to carry forward at this time. This ministry, rightly performed, will bring rich blessings to the church.*[62]

The effect of this kind of *building*[1129] is <u>expansion</u>. The church will grow when medical missionary work is performed as God intended it to be.

> [Medical missionary work] *is a part of the gospel message, and must receive recognition. It is the heaven-ordained means of finding entrance to the hearts of people. It is the duty of our church members in every place to follow the instruction of the Great Teacher. The gospel message is to be preached in every city; for this is in accordance with*

---

[62] Ellen G. White, *Testimonies for the Church, vol. 6* (Mountain View, CA: Pacific Press, 1901), p. 266, emphasis mine.

the example of Christ and His disciples. Medical missionaries are to seek patiently and earnestly to reach the higher classes. If this work is faithfully done, professional men will become trained evangelists.[63]

Combine medical missionary work with the proclamation of the third angel's message. Make regular, organized efforts to lift the church members out of the dead level in which they have been for years. Send out into the churches workers who will live the principles of health reform. <u>Let those be sent who can see the necessity of self-denial in appetite, or they will be a snare to the church.</u> See if the breath of life will not then come into your churches.[64]

So, Benaiah's name associates us with <u>Egyptian deliverance, healthful living</u>, and a <u>final, expansive work</u> of God. Prophetically, it projects us to the last days, God's remnant people, the final proclamation of the Gospel, the third angel's message, and medical missionary work.

Benaiah's father's name, Jehoiada, adds even more depth.

Jehoiada, *knowledge of the Lord*, is also a contraction of two Hebrew words—"Jehovah" (Strong's H3068) and "to know" (Strong's H3045). This use of the name of God was first introduced in Genesis 2:4, during the second rendering of Creation Week, and is attached to Elohim,[430] the Creator Gods of Genesis 1. "Jehovah[3068]" adds the dimension of JUDGE (one who is able to discern what is needed) and FACILITATOR (one who is able to do or make what is needed). The Hebrew word for "to know" (properly, to ascertain by seeing) puts emphasis on knowledge that comes <u>through the senses</u>, through <u>experience</u>.

"And the eyes of them both were opened, and they knew[3045] that they were naked; and they sewed fig leaves together, and made themselves aprons" (Gen. 3:7).

"And Adam knew[3045] Eve his wife; and she conceived, and bare Cain, and said, I have gotten a man from the LORD" (Gen. 4:1).

Whatever Benaiah did or represents should also include this aspect of his father, for Benaiah is rarely mentioned without his father's name attached. Benaiah's father knew God by experience, the Great I AM, and apparently instilled this knowledge in his son, who became one of David and Solomon's most highly respected warriors.

---

[63] Ellen G. White, *Medical Ministry* (Mountain View, CA: Pacific Press, 1932), p. 241, emphasis mine.

[64] Ellen G. White, *Testimonies for the Church, vol. 6* (Mountain View, CA: Pacific Press, 1901), p. 267, emphasis mine.

No line is to be drawn between the genuine medical missionary work and the gospel ministry. These two must blend. They are not to stand apart as separate lines of work. They are to be joined in an inseparable union, even as the hand is joined to the body. Those in our institutions are to give evidence that they understand their part in the genuine gospel medical missionary work. A solemn dignity is to characterize genuine medical missionaries. They are to be men who understand and know God and the power of His grace.[65]

The great outpouring of the Spirit of God, which lightens the whole earth with His glory, will not come until we have an enlightened people, that know by experience what it means to be laborers together with God. When we have entire, wholehearted consecration to the service of Christ, God will recognize the fact by an outpouring of His Spirit without measure; but this will not be while the largest portion of the church are not laborers together with God.[66]

KABZEEL

Where we are born and spend our formative years often has an effect on what we become. This was implied in Nathaniel's comment about where Jesus grew up.

"Philip found Nathaniel and said to him, We have found Him of whom Moses wrote in the Law and the Prophets, Jesus of Nazareth, the son of Joseph. And Nathaniel said to him, Can there be any good thing come out of Nazareth? Philip said to him, Come and see" (John 1:45–46, MKJV).

Apparently, there is also something significant in Benaiah's birthplace and hometown of Kabzeel. Kabzeel was a city of Judah, lying in the southernmost portion of the Promised Land, close to Egypt. Judah, represented by a lion, and characterized by his use of his hands, was placed in the lead position among the twelve tribes. As we learn in the study of the sanctuary, the south is associated positively with victory over internal forces, over powers of the carnal nature. Temperate living was the style—if these people lived what their name indicates. And Benaiah was considered a "valiant man" of Kabzeel, suggesting his positive response to these influences. As a Judahite, he also was very capable with his hands and a leader.

---

[65] Ellen G. White, *Medical Ministry* (Mountain View, CA: Pacific Press, 1932), p. 250, emphasis mine.
[66] Ellen G. White, *Christian Service* (Hagerstown, MD: Review and Herald, 1925), p. 253, emphasis mine.

The name Kabzeel is translated as "the congregation of God" or "whom God collects." We get the idea that the city was a favorite gathering of those who honored and worshipped Jehovah—like the atmosphere attending a camp meeting. This could also have been an influence on the young lad.

PROXIMITY TO EGYPT

Benaiah appears to be well-groomed in the knowledge and ways of God. He came from a powerful tribe, grew up in a community and in a family devoted to God, not far from Egypt. It's likely being so close to that heathen kingdom and so devoted to the God of heaven, a great sensitivity could have been nurtured against Egyptian influences. Benaiah may have been able to detect Egyptian falsehoods and deceptions much more readily than someone growing up far removed from the clay-kingdom's borders.

LION THEME

Additional information is given about this warrior for God, that we might be well instructed in the one taking on the giant from Egypt.

Benaiah was a Judahite. His tribe was represented by a lion, the king of beasts. John the Revelator refers to our last-day Deliverer as *the Lion of the tribe of Judah*. Benaiah describes those who most closely reflect Christ.

> **And I saw a book on the right of Him sitting on the throne, written inside and on the back, sealed with seven seals. And I saw a mighty angel proclaiming with a loud voice, Who is worthy to open the book and to loosen its seals? And no one in Heaven, nor on the earth, nor under the earth, was able to open the book or to look at it. And I wept very much, because no one was found worthy to open and to read the book, nor to look at it. And one of the elders said to me, Do not weep. Behold, the Lion of the tribe of Judah, the Root of David, has prevailed to open the book and to loose the seven seals of it. And I looked, and lo, In the midst of the throne and of the four living creatures, amidst the elders, a Lamb stood, as if it had been slain, having seven horns and seven eyes, which are the seven Spirits of God sent forth into all the earth. And He came and took the book out of the right hand of Him sitting on the throne.** (Rev. 5:1–7, MKJV)

The lion theme continues. The record says Benaiah killed two lion-like men of Moab—"lions of God" the Hebrew says. This is not describing two hairy, wild, and crazy men who had lost their senses, becoming more animal than human. On the contrary, the emphasis in Hebrew indicates that the men were <u>zealous and heroic</u>, fighting for a divine cause, though, in this case, misguided. They, too, must have been leaders and defenders. But they were Moabites, incestuous sons of Lot resulting from an endearing relationship with Sodom. Likely their leadership was driven by sensuality and violence. However, they were not a match for Benaiah.

This suggests that the son of Jehoiada was devoted to the true God and earlier gained victory over the carnal nature, like the apostle Paul did.

"But I keep under my body, and bring it into subjection: lest that by any means, when I have preached to others, I myself should be a castaway" (1 Cor. 9:27).

To further impress us with Benaiah's abilities, we read that he also killed a lion in a pit on a snowy day. Here we have <u>natural</u> difficulties to contend with. Nothing is more calculated to arouse an animal's defensive nature than to be trapped in a confined area. Even less violent animals will fight for their life. Their natural fear of man is replaced by self-preservation. What further complicates the fray is the weather. If you have ever walked in snow, you know that it takes much more energy than walking on dry ground. And ice makes it even worse. Also, cold weather encourages us to bundle up more, restricting our freedom of movement. Benaiah, no doubt, had to face these natural difficulties when confronting this violent and strong animal. Yet, even here, God's man wins.

Benaiah, by the grace of God, not only gained control over his carnal nature, he also showed superiority over the godless forces of nature. It reminds me of a statement Christ's disciples made when He calmed the storm.

"But the men marveled, saying, What kind of man is this, that even the winds and the sea obey him!" (Matt. 8:27, MKJV).

The first Adam was given authority over all nature. He forfeited it by taking of the tree of knowledge of good and evil.

"Thou madest him to have dominion over the works of thy hands; thou hast put all things under his feet ... the beasts of the field; the fowl of the air ... and whatsoever passeth through the paths of the seas" (Ps. 8:6–8).

"Though formed from the dust, Adam was "the son of God." He was placed, as God's representative, over the lower orders of being. They cannot

understand or acknowledge the sovereignty of God, yet they were made capable of loving and serving man."[67]

> *Adam was appointed by God to be monarch of the world, under the supervision of the Creator. "God said, Let us make man in Our image, after our likeness, and let him have dominion over the fish of the sea, and over the fowl of the air, and over the cattle, and over all the earth, and over every creeping thing that creepeth upon the earth. So God created man in His own image, in the image of God created He him."*[68]

Christ, the second Adam (1 Cor. 15:45), regained it.

"[A]nd that dominion, once consigned to Adam over the creation, and forfeited by him" (Genesis 1:26; 3:17), *shall be given to Jesus. He shall be king over all the earth."*[69]

Is this aspect of Benaiah—his power over the flesh as well as inclement forces of nature—suggesting God's final representatives, the 144,000, may also be reinstated with the same authority Adam forfeited and Jesus reclaimed? This is highly suggested in the fact that they, those who got victory over the beast, his image, his mark, and even his number, sing the song of Moses and the Lamb (Rev. 15:2–3). When Moses struck the rock the second time, he brought forth water. But God did not authorize him to do it! Moses misused a power entrusted to him of God and was chastised by Jehovah for so doing.

"And the LORD spake unto Moses and Aaron, Because ye believed me not, to sanctify me in the eyes of the children of Israel, therefore ye shall not bring this congregation into the land which I have given them" (Num. 20:12).

Apparently, the Benaiahs of the last days will not so misuse their entrusted powers but do only as the Lamb did.

"Believest thou not that I am in the Father, and the Father in me? the words that I speak unto you I speak not of myself: but the Father that dwelleth in me, he doeth the works" (John 14:10).

Putting This All Together

We learn that Benaiah was called of God for a particular mission. His name speaks of an end-time deliverer from Egyptian bondage and points to a

---

[67] Ellen G. White, *Patriarchs and Prophets* (Mountain View, CA: Pacific Press, 1890), p. 45, emphasis mine.

[68] Ellen G. White, "The Marriage in Cana of Galilee," *The Signs of the Times*, August 30, 1899, emphasis mine.

[69] Ellen G. White, *The Great Controversy 1888* (Mountain View, CA: Pacific Press, 1888), p. 359, emphasis mine.

special work God will do just before He comes. As we look at Benaiah's family and where he grew up, we see that the LORD had well-groomed him in spiritual life and warfare. He most likely grew up in a family who feared God and in a community that worshipped Him. And if names and abilities mean anything, Benaiah, must have included healthful living as part of his worship. We can also expect that discernment was a vital part of his education, for being so close to Egypt, he undoubtedly learned much about their gods and life, and was able to contrast that with the fuller and richer life the great I AM offers. Like with David, before facing the giant, Benaiah was prepared by lesser battles.

To have mastery over natural difficulties as well as unnatural ones (those devised by cunning minds and fearless warriors), Benaiah must have learned self-mastery in ways few knew in his day—an important training for medical missionaries and God's final remnant.

> *The body is to be brought into subjection to the higher powers of the being. The passions are to be controlled by the will, which is itself to be under the control of God.... Intellectual power, physical stamina, and the length of life depend upon immutable laws. Through obedience to these laws, man may stand conqueror of himself, conqueror of his own inclinations, conqueror of principalities and powers of "the rulers of the darkness of this world," and of "spiritual wickedness in high places."*[70]

THE ROD

Benaiah, we're told, had only a shepherd's staff with him when he fought the Egyptian. The KJV uses "staff," but the Hebrew word should actually be translated as "rod" (Strong's H7626). He was either not planning on a battle at that time or depending solely on God's help, understanding what the rod represented. In Psalm 23:4 ("thy rod and thy staff they comfort me"), the word for "rod" is the same word for what Benaiah carried with him to the battle. Shepherds used the rod for ruling, taking inventory, writing, walking, fighting, punishing, etc. In a prophecy of the coming Messiah, it was the rod (scepter) that would not depart from Israel until He came. *The rod*[7626] *was an emblem of authority.*

"**The sceptre**[7626] **shall not depart from Judah, nor a lawgiver from between his feet, until Shiloh come; and unto him shall the gathering of the people be**" (Gen. 49:10).

---

[70] Ellen G. White, *God's Amazing Grace* (Washington, DC: Review and Herald, 1973), p. 256, emphasis mine.

"I shall see him, but not now: I shall behold him, but not nigh: there shall come a Star out of Jacob, and a Sceptre[7626] shall rise out of Israel" (Num. 24:17).

With the emblem of <u>God's authority</u> in his hand, and obedient to its precepts, Benaiah approached the giant. This was the source of Benaiah's power. The rod of God was also the source of Moses' power in confronting the pharaoh of Egypt.[71] Could it also symbolize that which the 144,000 use at the end of time to help deliver God's people from the powers of clay and iron (the Sabbath, which represents the whole law)? Hmmm.

Armed with "Bible truth," Benaiah confronted the Egyptian, took the spear out of the Egyptian's hand, and slew him with his own weapon. This detail is very significant when we consider its application to the last day work.

> *The word of God in His law is binding upon every intelligent mind. The truth for this time, the third angel's message, is to be proclaimed with a loud voice, meaning with increasing power, as we approach the great final test. This test must come to the churches in connection with the true medical missionary work, a work that has the Great Physician to dictate and preside in all it comprehends. Under the great Head we are to present God's word requiring obedience to the system of Bible truth, which is a system of authority and power, convicting and converting the conscience. The demand of the Word to obedience is a life-and-death question.*[72]

This is a very important point. The "rod" is not just the Bible and the Bible alone, but it also implies OBEDIENCE to every word in it. "[H]ere are they that keep" (Rev. 14:12). It was Benaiah's faithfulness to its precepts that gave him power over the Egyptian and disarmed him of his powerful spear.

THE BATTLE ... IN TYPE

From the description of the giant, the position of the clay in the feet of Daniel 2's image, and the implications in the names and descriptions associated with Benaiah, the victorious warrior, the battle appears to be prophetic of the last days. It will be a spiritual, mental, and physical battle, involving concepts of true education, medical missionary work, and the third angel's message.

---

[71] Exodus 4:2.
[72] Ellen G. White, *Manuscript Releases, vol. 10* (Silver Spring, MD: Ellen G. White Estate, 1990), p. 314, emphasis mine.

What is soon coming upon us? Seducing spirits are coming in. If God has ever spoken by me, you will before long hear of a wonderful science—a science of the devil. Its aim will be to make of no account God and Jesus Christ whom He has sent. Some will exalt this false science, and through them Satan will seek to make void the law of God. Great miracles will be performed in the sight of men in behalf of this wonderful science.[73]

In this final battle, we see a confrontation between the champions of good and evil. What makes it particularly difficult for God's people is that their opponents were once their **friends**, protecting them and favoring them with the choicest of blessings, helping them to gain in strength and numbers, at times educating their children, giving medical assistance, providing family and business counseling, and occasionally even sharing pulpits. *"Surely they wouldn't turn against us!"*

Jesus longed for some support from His friends during His last hours, but none was given. Even Judas, who appeared as the most favored of the disciples (from the world's perspective), betrayed Him with a kiss. And where were His beloved John and faithful Peter?

Our Savior had to depend solely on His relationship with His heavenly Father, and Him alone. And so it will be with God's remnant. Jesus fought alone. Benaiah fought alone. And so must we. Egypt is a turncoat and cannot be trusted! As God led us into Egypt to strengthen and grow, He will also deliver us from Egypt in the final hours.

SUMMARY

The Egyptian giant represents a worldly system that appears in all respects to be a safe haven for God's people in times of need. The giant looks goodly and attractive. Few recognize him as a threat, and in the beginning, he most likely isn't. He appears quasi-religious, offering protection, sustenance, healing, and inspiration. He has wormed his way into our hearts, homes, and pulpits. However, because of his enchantment with mystic powers, this friendly system turns deceptively dangerous. As he rejects the mercies and merits of God through His only begotten Son, this giant transforms from a goodly giant into a beastly power. Through him, a false science is introduced as a weapon against God and truth (the "weaver's beam"). His weapon represents the finest **trappings** the world has for building

---

[73] Ellen G. White, *Selected Messages, book 3* (Washington, DC: Review and Herald, 1980), p. 408, emphasis mine.

character and extending (mortal) life, "proving" its validity with miracles and healings. Soul enslavement results to his unwary followers.

The second beast of Revelation 13:11–18 is described in the same way the first beast is (same Greek word in Strong's Concordance—G2342): *therion*, a *dangerous animal:* (venomous, wild) beast. We know this beast portrays the United States, which became a refuge for God's persecuted people, but John applied a word describing the *end characteristics* of this nation, when it transforms into its natural state after turning away from God's directives. It will not be a religious power but a mystic political one, as Egypt became in Moses' day, who cooperates with a renegade Christian church to form a world power, antagonistic to the Creator God (Rev. 14:7).

But God has His appointed means to bring deliverance. He gives birth to a remnant people and protects and strengthens them against the influences of Egypt. He then directs them into true education and health reform and commissions them to become gospel medical missionary workers all over the world.

"True conversion to the message of present truth embraces conversion to the principles of health reform."[74]

The remnant have been nurtured in the fear and love of God, skilled in spiritual warfare, and honed in dealing with natural and human challenges, especially those that are aimed against the final message. Their eyes have been anointed with the precious, holy eyesalve of Revelation 3:18, allowing them to see past the Egyptian's facade.

"The eyesalve is that wisdom and grace which enables us to discern between the evil and the good, and to detect sin under any guise."[75]

And valiant for the truth, obedient to all God's commands and armed with the authority of God, His Word (law), they confront the giant. This is too much for the goodly giant. He has no weapon against the Word of God. He is disarmed and is finally destroyed by his own weapon (the "exposion" of the "wonderful science" he used to deceive the world). Here we see the purpose, power, and divine potential of true medical missionary work.

> *How slow men are to understand God's preparation for the day of His power! God works today to reach hearts in the same way that He worked when Christ was upon this earth. In reading the word of God, we see that Christ brought medical missionary work into His*

---

[74] Arthur L. White, *Ellen White: Woman of Vision* (Review and Herald, 2000), p. 509, emphasis mine.

[75] Ellen G. White, *Testimonies for the Church, vol. 4* (Mountain View, CA: Pacific Press, 1881), p. 88, emphasis mine.

ministry. Cannot our eyes be opened to discern Christ's methods? Cannot we understand the commission He gave to His disciples and to us?"[76]

"The medical missionary work is as the right arm of the third angel's message which must be proclaimed to a fallen world."[77]

"When properly conducted, the health work is an entering wedge, making a way for other truths to reach the heart. When the third angel's message is received in its fullness, health reform will be given its place in the councils of the conference, in the work of the church, in the home, at the table, and in all the household arrangements. Then the right arm will serve and protect the body."[78]

As a result of his timely defense of the kingdom, many souls will be added to God's family.

"We must take advantage of the means that the Lord has placed in our hands for the carrying forward of medical missionary work. Through this work infidels will be converted. Through the wonderful restorations taking place in our sanitariums, souls will be led to look to Christ as the Great Healer of soul and body."[79]

In the confrontation between the false science promoted by the Egyptian giant (which leads away from God) and true education heralded by the Benaiahs of the last days (which leads to God), it will be shown that ...

> *And in the days of the kingdoms of iron and clay, God will establish His kingdom on this earth, a kingdom of stone cut out of His holy mountain without [human] hands. And that kingdom will break in pieces the earthly manifestations of iron, brass, clay, silver, and gold. And then only righteousness and truth will reign supreme.*

> *God is the foundation of everything. All true science is in harmony with His works; all true education leads to obedience to His government.*

---

[76] Ellen G. White, *Medical Ministry* (Mountain View, CA: Pacific Press, 1932), p. 246, emphasis mine.

[77] Ellen G. White, *Counsels on Health* (Mountain View, CA: Pacific Press, 1923), p. 331, emphasis mine.

[78] Ellen G. White, *Manual for Canvassers* (Mountain View, CA: Pacific Press, 1902), p. 45, emphasis mine.

[79] Ellen G. White, *Medical Ministry* (Mountain View, CA: Pacific Press, 1932), p. 328, emphasis mine.

> *Science opens new wonders to our view; she soars high, and explores new depths; but she brings nothing from her research that conflicts with divine revelation. Ignorance may seek to support false views of God by appeals to science, but the book of nature and the written word shed light upon each other. We are thus led to adore the Creator and to have an intelligent trust in His word.*[80]

And in the days of the kingdoms of iron and clay, God will establish His kingdom on this earth, a kingdom of stone cut out of His holy mountain without [human] hands. And that kingdom will break in pieces the earthly manifestations of iron, brass, clay, silver, and gold. And then only righteousness and truth will reign supreme.

We live in the last days. There is a great work for God and us to do yet—in our hearts as well as in the world—a work that requires a thorough understanding of God's revealed will and thought. The better we understand His Word, the more intelligently we can cooperate with His leading. Let us not be duped by educators or counselors who purport to teach Christian virtues and doctrines but in effect draw from the tree of knowledge of good and evil, appealing to our unsanctified senses and increasing our self-sufficiency. God's program develops true gospel medical missionaries.

BREAKING THE GIANT CODE

These giants have been with us for a long, long time. Their effect on God's people has always been the same—to separate them from their Creator/Redeemer and make of none effect His divine law. The renegade prophet Balaam got it right: disobedience destroys.

> *Balaam knew that the prosperity of Israel depended upon their obedience to God, and that there was no way to cause their overthrow but by seducing them into sin. He now decided to secure Balak's favor by advising the Moabites of the course to be pursued to bring a curse upon Israel. He immediately returned to the land of Moab and laid his plans before the king. The Moabites themselves were convinced that so long as Israel remained true to God, He would be their shield. The plan proposed by Balaam was to separate them from God by enticing them into idolatry. If they could be led to engage in the licentious worship of Baal and Ashtaroth, their omnipotent Protector would become their*

---

[80] Ellen G. White, *Patriarchs and Prophets* (Mountain View, CA: Pacific Press, 1890), pp. 115-116, emphasis mine.

enemy, and they would soon fall a prey to the fierce, warlike nations around them.[81]

Daniel tells us that the five components that make up the giant image in chapter 2 remain intact until God sets up His own kingdom. Revelation supports this, for there we see the spirit of the first kingdom, Babylon, alive and well, as well as the last kingdoms of iron and clay still determined to allure and force God's people into disobedience.

We often find ourselves impotent to overcome these mighty giants on our own. Our only safety is to be faithful to the only true God and believe in His only begotten Son.[82] As God helped King David fight their counterparts thousands of years ago, He will help us today. He is the Rock that finally destroys this fearsome image.

Praise God! The giant code has been broken! Now we see the behemoths in their true nature and exactly how each can be overthrown. But victory is not in knowledge alone. The triumphs yet ahead are gained only by trusting in God, believing His prophets, and being obedient to His Word.

Let's go forth to conquer! His grace is sufficient.

Hopefully this study will inspire the serious student to mine the Word of God and see for him/herself the gems of truth long covered over by the dust of worldliness, humanism, deceit, and error.

> *The Bible contains all the principles that men need to understand in order to be fitted either for this life or for the life to come. And these principles may be understood by all. No one with a spirit to appreciate its teaching can read a single passage from the Bible without gaining from it some helpful thought. But the most valuable teaching of the Bible is not to be gained by occasional or disconnected study. Its great system of truth is not so presented as to be discerned by the hasty or careless reader. Many of its treasures lie FAR BENEATH THE SURFACE, and can be obtained only by diligent research and continuous effort. The truths that go to make up the great whole must be searched out and gathered up, "here a little, and there a little." Isaiah 28:10. When thus searched out and brought together, they will be found to be perfectly fitted to one another.*[83]

---

[81] Ibid., p. 451, emphasis mine.
[82] John 17:3.
[83] Ellen G. White, *Education* (Mountain View, CA: Pacific Press, 1903), p. 123, emphasis mine.

BIBLIOGRAPHY

Erdman, Lynn. "Laughter Therapy for Patients with Cancer." Taylor & Francis Online. https://1ref.us/1sb.

Jamieson, D.D. Robert, A.R. Fausset, and David Brown. "Commentary Critical and Explanatory on the Whole Bible." Study Light. https://1ref.us/1se.

Junkins, Enda. "Welcome to Laughter Therapy Enterprises." Laughter Therapy Enterprises. https://1ref.us/1sc.

Kersten, Holger. JSTOR. https://1ref.us/1sa.

McKeever, Vicky. "Why laughter can make you more productive at work." CNBC. https://1ref.us/1sd.

Sauder, Brian. *Prosperity with a Purpose*, House to House Publications, 2003.

Strong, James. *Dictionaries of Hebrew and Greek Words taken from Strong's Exhaustive Concordance*, S.T.D., L.L.D. Published in 1890, public domain.

White, Arthur L. *Ellen White: Woman of Vision*. Review and Herald Publishing Association, 2000.

White, Ellen G. "A Missionary Education." *The Review and Herald*, February 6, 1908.

———. *Christian Experience and Teachings of Ellen G. White*. Mountain View, CA: Pacific Press Publishing Association, 1922.

———. *Christian Service*. Hagerstown, MD: Review and Herald Publishing Association, 1925.

———. *Christ's Object Lessons*. Washington, DC: Review and Herald Publishing Association, 1900.

———. *Counsels on Health*. Mountain View, CA: Pacific Press Publishing Association, 1923.

———. *Early Writings*. Washington, DC: Review and Herald Publishing Association, 1882.

———. *Education*. Mountain View, CA: Pacific Press Publishing Association, 1903.

———. *God's Amazing Grace*. Washington, DC: Review and Herald Publishing Association, 1973.

———. *Manual for Canvassers*. Mountain View, CA: Pacific Press Publishing Association, 1902.

———. *Manuscript Releases. Vol. 10*. Silver Spring, MD: Ellen G. White Estate, 1990.

———. *Maranatha*. Washington, DC: Review and Herald Publishing Association, 1976.

———. *Medical Ministry*. Mountain View, CA: Pacific Press Publishing Association, 1932.

———. "Principle Never to be Sacrificed for Peace." *The Bible Echo*, March 26, 1894.

———. *Prophets and Kings*. Mountain View, CA: Pacific Press Publishing Association, 1917.

———. *SDA Bible Commentary. Vol. 4*. Washington, DC: Review and Herald Publishing Association, 1955.

———. *Selected Messages. Book 3*. Washington, DC: Review and Herald Publishing Association, 1980.

———. *Steps to Christ*. Mountain View, CA: Pacific Press Publishing Association, 1892.

———. "Strength in Humility." *The Youth's Instructor*, January 29, 1903.

———. *Testimonies for the Church. Vol. 2*. Mountain View, CA: Pacific Press Publishing Association, 1871.

———. *Testimonies for the Church. Vol. 4.* Mountain View, CA: Pacific Press Publishing Association, 1881.

———. *Testimonies for the Church. Vol. 5.* Mountain View, CA: Pacific Press Publishing Association, 1889.

———. *Testimonies for the Church. Vol. 6.* Mountain View, CA: Pacific Press Publishing Association, 1901.

———. *The Adventist Home.* Hagerstown, MD: Review and Herald Publishing Association, 1952.

———. *The Desire of Ages.* Mountain View, CA: Pacific Press Publishing Association, 1898.

———. *The Faith I Live By.* Washington, DC: Review and Herald Publishing Association, 1958.

———. *The Great Controversy.* Mountain View, CA: Pacific Press Publishing Association, 1911.

———. *The Great Controversy 1888.* Mountain View, CA: Pacific Press Publishing Association, 1888.

———. "The Marriage in Cana of Galilee." *The Signs of the Times*, August 30, 1899.

———. *The Ministry of Healing.* Mountain View, CA: Pacific Press Publishing Association, 1905.

———. *The Spirit of Prophecy.* Battle Creek, MI: Seventh-day Adventist Publishing Association, 1878.

———. *The Story of Redemption.* Hagerstown, MD: Review and Herald Publishing Association, 1947.

———. "The Word Made Flesh." *The Signs of the Times,* May 3, 1899.

TEACH Services, Inc.
P U B L I S H I N G

We invite you to view the complete
selection of titles we publish at:
www.TEACHServices.com

We encourage you to write us
with your thoughts about this,
or any other book we publish at:
info@TEACHServices.com

TEACH Services' titles may be purchased in
bulk quantities for educational, fund-raising,
business, or promotional use.
bulksales@TEACHServices.com

Finally, if you are interested in seeing
your own book in print, please contact us at:
publishing@TEACHServices.com
We are happy to review your manuscript at no charge.

www.ingramcontent.com/pod-product-compliance
Lightning Source LLC
Chambersburg PA
CBHW070557160426
43199CB00014B/2534